Confessions of a Yo-Yo Dieter

Confessions of a Yo-Yo Dieter

How I overcame obsessive dieting and created a fun life with food

Katheryn Gronauer

Copyright © 2018 Katheryn Gronauer

All rights reserved.

Without limiting the rights under copyright reserved, no part of this book, including both text and illustrations, may be reproduced, stored in or introduced into a retrieval system, or transmitted, in any form or by any means (electronic, mechanical, photocopying, recording or otherwise) without the prior written permission of both the copyright owner and the publisher of this book.

ISBN: 978-0-692-11371-4

Published and printed in [Tokyo, Japan]
First edition published in Japan by the author 2018

The author is a holistic health coach and is not a dietician, medical doctor, nutritionist, allergy specialist or macrobiotic counselor. The author does not provide dietary, medical, nutritional or allergy advice and this book is not intended to provide dietary, medical nutritional all allergy advice to the reader or anyone. The ideas, procedures and suggestions contained in this book are the author's own experiences and such ideas, procedures and suggestions are not to be used as a substitute for coaching and advice from a qualified dietician, medical doctor, nutritionist, allergy specialist or macrobiotic counselor. Anyone with dietary, medical, nutrition, allergy or health problems are advised to seek the guidance of a qualified dietician, medical doctor, nutritionist, allergy specialist or psychological professional before implementing the ideas, procedures, suggestions, and other approaches presented in this book. It is essential that a reader or anyone who has any reason to suspect serious illness in themselves or their family members or anyone else, seek appropriate dietary, medical, nutritional, allergy or psychological advice promptly. Neither the publisher nor the author is engaged in tendering professional advice or services to the reader or anyone. Neither the author nor the publisher shall be liable for or responsible for any loss, injury, or damage allegedly arising from any of the ideas, procedures, suggestions or other approaches presented in this book. The opinions expressed in this book represent the personal views of the author and not the publisher.

For any woman who has ever overindulged after a workout because she felt like she deserved it, who would rather wear a pair of tight pants in a smaller size than loose ones in a larger size, who has ever carried a tupperware with pre-measured portions of food to a social event, or faced any other diet dilemma of the sort...

This is for you.

I thank my family, the macrobiotic community, and the wonderful people I've met over the years who have invigorated a passion in me to create this book.

CONTENTS

Introduction	1
Part 1: My Story	11
Part 2: Cycles	37
Part 3: Lifestyle Change	63
Part 4: Macrobiotics	83
Part 5: Transitioning Your Diet	101
Part 6: Unexpected Discoveries	119
About Katheryn Gronauer	137

Introduction

As I'm writing this, I'm sitting in the Ritz Carlton Tokyo, sipping my favorite royal milk tea and munching on a buttery scone. Heels are high to the sky, dress is sleek, skin is clear, lips are red, hair is shiny. Feelin' good, lookin' good, eating yummy food.

Is this a dream? Sometimes I have to pinch myself, because it wasn't always like this.

In what feels like a past life (but not *too* long ago), I was 40 pounds overweight, had a face full of acne, and was a diet-obsessive-scale-stepping-cookie-bingeing yo-yo dieter. I'd analyze every crumb that went into my mouth, work out excessively at the gym, binge when no one was looking, and envy women who appeared to be able to look good without any effort.

But now? I'm that woman who can eat whatever she wants and not have weight issues. If you want to know how this is possible, then keep reading. This is the story of how I overcame obsessive dieting and created a fun life with food.

At the time of writing this, I'm 28 years old and living in Tokyo, Japan. My mother is Japanese and my father is American, so I spent my childhood growing up in Florida and visiting family in Tokyo each summer. My personal story starts from when I was living in the US and dieting at age 14, through when I reached my peak weight at boarding school in Connecticut, and finally explores Eastern holistic theories in college in Tokyo when I lost 40 pounds.

After my personal transformation, I became a certified health coach with a passion to share with you a different way of thinking that I hadn't been exposed to when I was living in the United States. To be clear, a health coach is someone you work with over time who helps you with the thought process and implementation of integrating health techniques into your lifestyle. In my case, I'm not a dietician, functional nutritionist or medical doctor.

In hindsight, I acknowledge that age 14 is a time when we're affected by hormonal changes and baby fat that can affect our weight. But I've found through meeting so many women of all ages with dieting histories not dissimilar to mine that the concerns we have about our bodies and our ability to change are the same. No matter your age or lifestyle challenges.

If you're reading this, you want your body to be different from how it is right now, and you're not sure how to get there. You're having a difficult time trusting that your body actually knows the right path.

Maybe you've already tried countless diets and are frustrated because you're not seeing the results you want. Maybe you feel like you know *what* to do, but haven't found the time nor the resources to make it happen. Perhaps you know what makes you feel good when you're *alone*, but you have no clue what to do when you're out of your element like dining out with friends or going on a vacation. Or you could be overwhelmed with so much conflicting diet information that you don't even know where to start.

I get it. But what exactly are we resisting about diets?

If we want to get healthy (and hot), then how come

following an exact formula creates so much angst? Shouldn't it create comfort and excitement if it's geared towards helping us reach our goals? I mean, if someone told you that there is an exact plan to help you make a million dollars, wouldn't you be excited to do the steps even if it's challenging?

The reason why we feel resistance is because diets make us question how we want to live our lives. They make us question what we value, what we feel we deserve, and what we feel makes life enjoyable. Food isn't just about fuel for the body; food is connected to us emotionally and socially.

For example, when I was growing up, going for afternoon tea with scones and reading a book was an experience I enjoyed with my family on a weekly basis. Taking the scones out of the picture made the experience feel incomplete. Scones had a deeper meaning than "just food" to me. They completed a picture of family bonding.

Diets make you question your social life, your comforts, your culture, and your relationships. Before you even embark on a diet, you're already wondering, "But what if...?"

I can eat salads but what if *I'm invited to a barbeque event this summer and there are only hamburgers and hotdogs?*

I can go gluten-free but what if *I'm dragged to a pizza party with work colleagues and can only have a refined white flour crust?!*

I can drink green smoothies but what if *I'm traveling on an airplane for business trips and can't make one?*

I can cut out sugar but what if *my mother in-law makes her famous brownies and gifts them to me and wants me to eat one in front of her?!*

We think of all the scenarios we'll face where we can't execute a diet without putting ourselves in an awkward situation where we'll either disappoint ourselves or disappoint other people.

Diets train you to think constantly about everything that goes into your mouth, when the goal you're *really* looking for is to be healthy without having to think at all.

How this book will help

In this book, I'm not going to tell you how I became a master at dieting. No, no, *no*. I'm going to share with you how I became free from *thinking* constantly about my diet.

We all have access to countless theories and advice on dieting, so the frustration you're experiencing is not from a lack of information, but from confusion around how all those copious parts fit together, along with maybe—just maybe—a resistance to the changes that need to happen for you to be happy with your body and enjoying life with food.

The only reason you've ever believed you've "fallen off the bandwagon" is because conventional health information isn't taught in a way that suits our modern lifestyles.

Our lifestyles—even though they might include a routine—have fluidity and uncertainty. That just doesn't integrate with strict meal plans based on cookie-cutter regimes. At the end of the day, you wind up feeling like you have to make a choice between engaging with the irregularities and celebrations of life, or to be rigid with your diet. You go into each new diet with a deep yearning that one day you'll be able to have what you want *after* you've met your goals.

I don't think it's necessarily the health industry's fault for giving us information in this way. If anything, we are the ones who ask industry experts to give us templates to follow, because they give us a feeling of relief and trust.

When life happens—as it inevitably does—we go on to beat ourselves up because we aren't in a position to stick to the plans we created a demand for in the first place.

Here's the thing: you're really the *only* person who understands how you feel.

Not any diet guru, health practitioner, fitness magazine, not even me. That means *your* voice and *your* experiences *matter*.

All of the ideas out there about health are tools to help you figure out what works best for you, so it's time to stop thinking of them as *rules* and start thinking of them as *opportunities* to learn more about yourself.

This book isn't an argument for the "best" diet. Instead, I've written *Confessions of a Yo-yo Dieter* to give you a completely new perspective around wellness and help you find the eating style that works for *you*, one that integrates with *your* chosen lifestyle. You're going to see more success once you're clear about how to *think*. That's the single most important outcome you can expect from reading this book.

At the end of the day, *you* are the final judge. You can become confident in making the best decisions for yourself, and I hope that my story will help you do just that.

What we'll cover

There are three rewards you'll gain from reading *Confessions of a Yo-yo Dieter*: a broad view of how seemingly independent health concepts interconnect, curiosity for developing a connection to your body, and confidence to make your own decisions.

One of the reasons why health concepts are challenging to understand is that we are missing the broad view on how they're supposed to fit together. The broad view is like the picture on the front of a puzzle box. Without it, all you have is a bunch of puzzle pieces that are important for creating a picture, but no understanding of how they're supposed to fit together nor what you're trying to create. You might be able to fit some pieces together on your own, but you can achieve so much more if you have an idea of what the final "health" picture is supposed to look like.

The second benefit you'll gain from reading this book is curiosity. The only way you'll ever understand what works for your body is if you explore a wide range of foods, cooking techniques, combinations, and wellness practices. You can't achieve a clear understanding of what works for your body if you start with restriction. There is no information that can be learned from losing access to food variety.

The third and final thing you'll get from this book is confidence in making your own decisions with a clear understanding of the role food plays in your life, both emotionally and socially. Our actions are driven by emotions and social scenarios, so it doesn't really make sense to only judge food as a source of fuel to be burned. Food is social, it's cultural, it's artistic, it's connected to nature, and it influences your emotions—from pleasure to memories and everything in between.

Despite this, most of the information we receive around food and health is explained in a logical, scientific way. Through the course of this book, we will bring in your senses and your environment so you can gain a better perspective on what to choose based on how you want to feel.

So that's what you can expect, but let's go back to the beginning, where it all started, my story of disconnection from food and how I found my way back.

Part 1: My Story

The day I knew my weight had gotten out of hand was when I discovered that my two rolls of back fat were bigger than my boobs.

My bra straps cut so deep into those rolls that for a split second, I considered wearing my bra on backwards. It was my back that needed the lift, after all.

Even though I was mortified at how wardrobe malfunctions seemed to relate to my body weight being distributed in the wrong places and not the wardrobe itself, my rock bottom moment was yet to come...

Hitting rock bottom

On a dreary winter day in Connecticut, I sank onto my dorm room bed holding an empty tray of peanut butter brownies and cried.

Ugly cried.

Crumbs clung to the corners of my lips and shirt, evidence of the brownies that were, and my stomach couldn't hold one more.

What was wrong *with me?*

I had planned to leave the freshly baked brownies in the boarding school common room to share with others in the dorm, saving just a piece for myself. As guilty as I felt about hogging the tray and eating the whole thing, deep down I knew that if my stomach was bigger, I would have kept eating.

The first time I had gone on an official diet was when I was 14. I had visited the doctor for an annual check-up and found out that I weighed more than the highest weight that was considered healthy for my height. Like most Americans who find themselves in that position, I went to Weight Watchers and started monitoring my food portions by counting Points. And it worked.

That is it worked as long as I was on it. The second I stopped counting Points, the weight would creep back on. It wasn't a fast gain. Just a bite of something here, a treat there, accumulating over time. From that point on, I labeled myself as someone who would have to monitor her eating habits constantly. I didn't trust that I wouldn't overdo it without *some* kind of system.

On that dorm room day, when I sat and cried over the empty tray of brownies, I felt like all the years of keeping my eating habits in check had spun out of control. The system was broken.

Most people describe a rock-bottom moment in a way that makes me imagine being stuck in a deep hole where you're not sure how you can climb back out. In my case, this moment felt more like an elastic band that snapped from being overstretched; I had pushed the boundaries of bingeing to the point where I'd stumbled over a line into territory where my eating habits were so out of control that I wasn't sure if it was even possible to bounce back. And *that* scared me more than any diet.

I knew something was wrong. I knew something had to change. It would take several more years before I figured out what that was. And yet, I set to work.

The days started out like this...

Each morning when I woke, before anything else, I'd grab my jiggly belly as I lay in bed, wondering if it felt a bit smaller than the night before. If it did, then that meant the workout I'd suffered through the previous afternoon must be working. If it felt the same or bigger, then I blamed my lack of progress on the bread I shouldn't have had with dinner the night before. Or on choosing pasta instead of a salad. Or on the spoonful of mayonnaise I hadn't accounted for...

I'd tip-toe across the cold bathroom tiles to the scale, stark naked and bowels emptied, wondering if I should shave a bit of underarm stubble to make sure the scale wouldn't be under the influence of the weight of unwanted hair. Some days, the number would be higher and I'd feel the kick in the gut. *I knew it.* Other days, I was *so* sure that I had gained weight, but as soon as I got on the scale I'd discover that I'd actually lost some. *Hey, I guess I had nothing to worry about!*

It didn't really matter if I *felt* good or bad, light or heavy. Progress was the only factor for me—and the scale held the results.

Zipping up my pants was like being on stage under a spotlight in the final moments of a game show. *Ladies and gentlemen, this is the moment of truth… Will they zip?!?* If they did, it was going to be a good day. If I had to hop around the room and then lie down on the bed to squeeze myself into them and barely get them closed, well, it'd still be an okay day as long as I didn't have to wear a larger size.

I'd open the fridge door and feel the cool air wake up my face as I debated what to have for breakfast. When I say "debated", I don't mean that I was wondering what I should have as much as arguing with myself that I *should* have the fruit when what I really wanted was a buttered bagel with milk tea. That was what I had grown up having for breakfast so it always felt weird to have anything else. I knew the fruit would be a healthier choice, except that I hated having something cold to eat first thing in the morning. I felt like the fruit was somehow "crunching" my stomach, and it left me feeling so hungry by lunch time. No matter which I chose, it felt lose-lose. If I had the fruit, I somehow felt like it gave me a ticket to be naughtier the rest of the day. If I had the bagel, I felt happy for the short moment as I was eating it, then felt guilty after.

Even though my eating habits felt like a constant struggle, I was pretty consistent about exercising. Each afternoon, I'd always do some kind of intense workout. Some days it was a workout dvd with high intensity interval training or kickboxing. Other days it was a couple hours of ice hockey training during the winter season at boarding school. And there were also those days where I'd hit the gym and make up my own workouts which consisted of awkwardly trying to lift a bunch of weights, running to the point of heavy sweating and exhaustion, and doing so many squats that I'd waddle back to my dorm room with legs that felt like over-cooked spaghetti.

I hated the thought of working out and also the process of exercising altogether, but it always made me feel like I was working towards my goal of losing weight and achieving my dream of looking good.

Nights were a lot harder when it came to controlling my eating habits. I'd be so hungry and exhausted from the gym that it was too easy to eat large portions of food (even if the meals were healthy). And I'd almost always justify having dessert because all the hard exercising I had done that day made me feel like I deserved a reward.

Why me?

I felt like the most diet-savvy of my friends, but I was also the heaviest. They didn't seem to care much about food in general. It was something they'd enjoy, but something they'd also easily forget. I couldn't understand my friends who could eat a few bites of a pizza and not feel like eating the rest. *How could they leave half behind?! Especially on cheat day?!* I remember when a friend told me once that she was craving an orange. *An orange?* I thought that the word "craving" was only something you'd use for naughty foods. I didn't think it was possible to crave something healthy.

It seemed like I was the only one dedicated to going to the gym or forcing myself to choose salad, yet I was the one struggling. The only answer I could think of was that I'd have to put in more effort to reap more reward, so I upped the intensity of my workouts or stayed longer on the treadmill. That effort looked like a lot of exercise and desperately trying everything to control my eating.

What I've tried

Specifically, my standard meals at boarding school went like this: for breakfast, lunch, and dinner, I made plain oatmeal and the salad bar my friend. I counted. I measured. I portioned. I did all of that good girl stuff. On top of that, I worked out at the gym for 1-2 hours per day. I'd do everything from high intensity interval training to running around a track to weight-lifting—anything that would help me build up a good sweat and make me feel like I was burning a lot of calories. Did I know anything about proper nutrition and exercise? Well, no, *though I thought I did*. But I was eating less and sweating like Miss Piggy, and that's all that mattered... *right?*

I spent a lot of time researching diets. I was obsessed with learning about neurotransmitters and metabolism, protein and the horrible effects of refined sugar. The body was like a mystery, full of undiscovered clues and interconnecting stories. I felt like a detective trying to figure out how everything linked up.

My poor roommate listened patiently to me as I explained how I thought she must have fibromyalgia (a fatigue syndrome) because she was so exhausted after studying late the night before for a test. And then, she supportively took photos of me in a bikini for my "before" shots—ones I swore to never show anyone, even if I could successfully create an "after". (They're still hiding on my hard drive, somewhere.) My oldest sister helped me cut out images of bodies I admired for motivational purposes along with different colors of construction paper so that I could paste them into a diet journal and feel extra motivated to "reach my goals this time". I even remember creating a "Support Katheryn's Weight Loss" Facebook group and inviting random school friends to join, with a message in the group description begging them not to lead me into temptation. The penalty for the ones who posted that I looked fine, didn't need to change, and should "love myself" as I was? Being removed from the group.

So yeah, I was pretty into this whole diet stuff. *But…* I also spent a lot of time trying to find loopholes, because in between meals and workouts? There was bingeing. *Lots* of bingeing. It went something like this:

If I worked out at the gym, I could reward myself with a cookie. *Burned off those calories, right?*

If I ate a salad, I could eat a cookie. *Everything in moderation, right?*

If I got a good grade at school, was praised at work, or felt any need of recognition for being awesome, I could eat a cookie. *I deserve a reward, right?*

Someone's being a jerk? Eat a cookie. Someone's uncle's friend's cousin's birthday, today? Celebrate with a cookie. Got 20 minutes left during a lunch break? Why not kill time with a cookie?

(As you can gather, my vice was cookies. *Chocolate chip* cookies. Do you know yours?)

I don't know why cookies meant so much to me at that stage of my life that I had to grasp onto them *so* dearly.

Perhaps it was merely the illusion that diets create where I felt I had to "give up" what I loved in order to make this whole health thing work. And since what I loved were cookies, cookies were the only thing I could think about while on any diet. Whether I could have a cookie on my diet plan was often the determining factor of whether I'd give that diet a try. As a result, I'm certain I wound up eating way more cookies *because* I was on a diet than I would have if I hadn't tried to diet in the first place.

As much as focusing on following rules, I was spending time trying to find loopholes around them. Heads up... That's not how you create healthy habits. That's how you create an eating disorder.

But you know what? Eating cookies wasn't even at the forefront of my angst with dieting. My angst came from the fact that I was *eating the salads* and *hitting the gym* and *still not* seeing any changes in my body. I flickered between being confused on what to do next and downright annoyed. Annoyed, because even though (as I've admitted) I was a cookie-binger, my vision of myself was of a hard-working, dedicated dieter.

I wasn't sitting on the sofa crying about my weight and wanting other people to do something about it for me. I was eating more salads and exercising way more than my slim friends. I was jealous that they seemed not to have to think about food nor do anything to stay slim, while I was huffing and puffing over here hungry, exhausted, and getting nowhere.

In my mind, I was a stellar, committed dieter who deserved a gold star (and rock-hard abs). I didn't think the cookies should have a significant impact on my body in comparison to all the effort I was putting in to shed the pounds.

Split personalities?

Have you ever felt like your mentality around dieting changes over the course of a week, each time you try a new diet? Some days I was so strict that I'd make sure to skim off the top layer of pasta that overflowed a cup when measuring portions. Other days I'd be like "embrace life!" and go to the buffet for seconds. I'd fluctuate back and forth between two different diet personality types.

See if you can identify yourself in these profiles. My experience went something like this:

The Go-Getter

You're a hard worker. You're logical. Everything has to make logical sense to you before you implement your strategy. You like knowing that if you could just follow a formula, you'll achieve your goals.

You're frustrated that you're putting in the work but not getting the results you imagine. Working hard has always worked for you in other aspects of your life. In school, you got rewarded with good grades. At work, you'll get promoted if you just go the extra mile. But the "hard work = results" mentality just doesn't seem to work for your diet.

You're more likely to avoid socializing if it's not your cheat day. And if you do wind up going out, you're worried that there won't be anything on the menu that would suit your meal plan, and you want to avoid being led into temptation. You figure that your current diet and workout plan are better than not doing anything at all because you fear that you'd look like a cow if you stopped doing both altogether.

You think that everyone else is programmed to be effortlessly slim, but not you. You? You're the one who has to work for it.

The Engager

You love to engage with other people. You may or may not

be a party person, but the point is you would rather interact with people than eat alone. And when you're with others, you just want to enjoy yourself without food boundaries!

You always plan and get excited for your diet adventure. You start on Monday, but have already given up by Wednesday. You go for lunch with work colleagues when invited, even though you've brought your own lunch to work. You work out more so that you can afford to eat more calories. You do quick-fixes like a fad diet or juice cleanse in between social outings.

It's hard for you to say no to others if they offer you foods that you don't want to eat. You wind up eating things you don't want, or eating more than you need, to avoid diet confrontation. You're scared that if you actually follow a diet plan, then you won't be able to socialize with friends. You think that your friends can eat pizza and still look good, but not you. You believe you could succeed at a diet if you really wanted to, but you "just love food too much".

I was pretty much a Go-Getter during the week and an Engager come the weekends. I'd fluctuate between trying to control every aspect of my schedule and food so that I could stick to my goal; then throwing up my hands at the end of the week saying "life is short!"—convinced I just needed to loosen up and enjoy life (with pizza).

The Dream

I always had this dream that I looked like a fancy diva, world traveler, and eater-of-all-cuisine. You know, like Miss Universe. Intellectual, gorgeous, cultured, worldly. *Effortless.*

Every image I had in my mind had some kind of connection to food—lounging with tea, clinking glasses of champagne with intellectuals, going to world renowned restaurants for anything from business discussions to celebrations. Much like you'd see on Instagram.

But diet and exercise got in the way of that dream. It seemed like if I were to take a trip to Italy, I'd have to skip the pasta and settle for salad. Then I'd go to France and skip the croissants to eat another salad. And say no to an afternoon tea invitation because I had to hit the gym. And clink glasses of sparkling water with intellectuals who were having champagne. My idea of what I had to give up in order to look how I wanted made my vision of life seem boring. Like a gorgeous woman on house arrest. I felt like I had to make a choice between eating what I wanted in order to create beautiful life memories, never mind the fat rolls and glorious zits, *or* giving all that up to look enviable in a bikini.

I'd leaf through fashion magazines and admire gorgeous women with slender bodies, and figured they were just lucky with genetics. I thought diets would make my problems go away but it made me overly analytical day in and day out. Attractive women didn't have to work at it, but I would have to for the *rest* of my life. *Sig*h.

Love yourself, right?

Back when I was at my highest weight and still today as I write this, there are these body positive messages floating around that say you need to "love yourself".

"Love yourself as much as you want to be loved."

"You're your biggest fan."

"If you don't love yourself, how can you expect others to love you?"

"The most important relationship is the one you have with yourself."

Back then, I remember looking in the mirror at bits of my body I was unhappy with and trying to practice saying the mantra "I love you" and... I felt like I was lying to myself. I felt like I was trying to *convince* myself to settle for a body I wasn't happy with. Like somehow, saying "I love you as you are" meant that I didn't have to put any effort into making positive changes because somehow that version of myself was supposed to be good enough.

How can you love yourself if you're not happy and want to change? I wondered. *How can you love yourself when you know you have so much potential to fulfill, and you know you want to be the best version of yourself? How can you settle for a body you're not happy with when that vision of the best version of yourself looks healthy, vibrant, and happy?*

I felt like diets were only training me to monitor and overanalyze myself, which was the opposite of the kind of relationship I wanted with my body. I wanted to be *free* from worrying about consequences. I wanted to be *free* from craving the foods that I knew were holding me back from feeling my best. I wanted to look in the mirror and not see a *different* person, but a raw, refined, diamond-outta-the-dust kinda version of myself.

And yet, not doing a diet at all seemed even scarier. How could I get healthy as well as become free from worrying about my weight *without* doing a diet? I felt like a life-long battle was ahead of me, but I was determined to fight it out.

Chatting with the nutritionist

Going back to my rock-bottom-brownie moment, when it was clear that something was wrong and had to change, I decided to do something about it when I heard a nutritionist talk at my school. I was *so* excited—I went to the lecture with the mindset that she was going to tell me the *one* piece of information that I was missing. You know, that one key piece to the puzzle that would make me have all the motivation in the world to get up at 5am and do a P90X home workout while simultaneously giving me the courage to shun chocolate chip cookies for the Rest. Of. My. Life. *Tell me, baby.*

But instead, she stuck with the basics: "Eat your vegetables, drink your water, and get your sleep." *What!?*

I'm pretty sure that you don't have to know much nutritional information to be aware that vegetables, water, and sleep are good for you. Why did we need to be reminded about such obvious stuff!? I didn't *want* to hear that sugar is bad. I already knew that. I wanted to hear *how* to overcome craving it in the first place. I didn't want to hear that I needed to exercise. I wanted to know *why* I wasn't getting smaller despite exercising way more than my slim friends. I didn't want to hear that I needed more sleep.

I wanted to know *how* I'm supposed to get more rest when I had so many responsibilities keeping me up late.

I left the lecture feeling like something was wrong with me, like everyone knew exactly what they had to do to get healthy, and that getting healthy was ridiculously simple, but that I was the only one struggling to make it work. But I still had hope, so I went to have a chat with the nutritionist privately to see if there was something I could do about my own situation. Maybe there was something *more* I could learn outside of the lecture.

I sat in her office in a stiff wooden chair. Looking down at my shoes and fidgeting with edge of my shirt, I revealed to her my deepest, darkest secret:

"*Yes…* it's true. I'm a real life cookie monster." (Well, my exact words were more subtle, but this is what I felt I should have said!) She listened. She *mmmhmm*-ed. And then she recommended that if I wanted to have a cookie, I *could*. But just a *little* one. Or maybe *half* of a regular one. "Everything in moderation."

Let me tell you something. When you're a cookie monster, "moderation" does not exist. I couldn't just have *one* cookie. It was all or nothing. Just passing by a plate of cookies planted an image in my mind that wouldn't go away until I got my fix. It didn't matter if it took 10 minutes or 10 *hours* of willpower—I knew subconsciously that I was going to wind up bingeing.

Plus, the problem with moderation is that I still felt guilty for having "bad" foods, even in tiny portions, even though I felt like I had deserved them. I felt like eating even a bite of cookie was sabotaging my efforts to exercise more or eat lots of vegetables, even though those efforts were to help me enjoy that very moment. Each indulgence made me question how committed I was to getting fit. Was it possible that I didn't truly want to change as much as I thought I did?

It took a lot of courage to reveal to her that I was a cookie monster. But I felt too ashamed to admit that I didn't think I could succeed at moderation. So I faked a smile of understanding, thanked her, and left the session feeling more nervous than when I had gone in.

Now, you might not have as serious an eating issue as I had. Maybe you generally eat well and just want to feel more confident with your choices. That's fine. But I wanted to share with you that point in my story because it shows just how bad things can get if you don't understand how to approach your health. Since meeting with the nutritionist that day, I spent a few more years struggling with my diet, but let's fast forward to the part where I started turning it all around.

Turning it all around... in Japan

Before I get into any depth about my weight loss, a quick word on what this is not. This is not about sushi, green tea, and kimonos. This is not about the details of the diet I followed. The lessons I learned can apply to you *wherever you're located*. I aim to show you how completely changing my context and placing myself in a new environment gave me a fresh perspective, and that's where I learned what works, what doesn't, and how to turn it around.

I wandered the streets of Tokyo's shopping district, weaving my way through crowds of slender, stylish women. How were these women *so* slim despite eating a wide range of foods? *Lucky bitches.* I'd walk past cafes and see pairs of women at every table gossiping about their weeks over tea and strawberry shortcake. I'd go out for dinner and see women dining all around me eating generous portions of beef. And every day when I'd commute or run an errand, nowhere in sight was there a woman power-walking in tight spandex with a two-liter bottle of water tucked under her arm like I had typically seen in the US. Their diets seemed to be much more enjoyable with an extensive variety of options, and they didn't seem to opt for sweat-drenching workouts. *What was going on, here?!* It made me wonder: if we all had the same information about health, how come these women made being healthy look so effortless and enjoyable?

In addition to what I observed in the streets, I noticed that my body seemed to be changing naturally as well. I couldn't figure out why. I had lost about 10 pounds within the first few months of living in Tokyo. While I still had a strong sweet tooth, I had taken a hiatus from obsessively monitoring my diet. I was too busy exploring the new place I was living in and being stimulated by my environment.

Before coming to Japan, I had read that the Japanese diet was healthy, but I didn't feel that sushi and green tea were the answers to their ability to enjoy food and stay slim. Heck, I wasn't even eating much fish myself nor drinking green tea, yet my body was changing. There had to be something more to it. But what?

I didn't know what they were doing differently, but I did know that I wanted what they had: enjoying food and looking good. So, I started to research.

One book changed everything

One day, on my way home, I got distracted window-shopping and found myself wandering through a department store. I made my way past countless shops showing off the latest fall trends and buried myself deep into the back of a bookstore in the vegetarian cookbook section. I wasn't a vegetarian, but since I was living on my own for the first time, I wanted to learn how to cook a bit more—especially healthy recipes with lots of vegetables. I figured that the vegetarian section would have the most veggie recipes. But instead of typical vegetarian recipe books, there were several other books that caught my eye. Each of them showed detailed explanations about a healing concept called "macrobiotics". I had no clue what this "macrobiotics" was, but I was instantly intrigued. I found diagrams of foods and portions that looked *exactly* like how I had been eating since arriving in Japan, with explanations of how this method of eating was supposed to bring *balance* to the body.

These books seemed to suggest that our health was directly affected and *guided* by nature, and that eating and living in a way that harmonized with nature would create balance and harmony within our bodies. *Huh. Interesting.*

I had never heard of diet being explained in this way. Most books I had ever come across involved deep explanations on things like proteins and metabolism and "devilish carbs" and meal plans. This one was different. It was more a *philosophical* explanation of how to eat in a way that would create both physical and emotional balance. As different as the concepts sounded, it was the first thing I had read that seemed so... *normal.* Natural, even. Whereas most diets spoke to my logical brain, this one spoke to my heart.

The more I read, the more I couldn't help but wonder...
Have I been thinking about health all wrong?

Here's what I discovered over the following years of delving into holistic health.

Part 2: Cycles

When we are born, all we know about the body comes from our instinct. Nobody is born with the scientific knowledge of what happens in the body. You were no different.

You had to *learn* what protein is. You had to *learn* what carbs are. You had to *learn* what vitamins and minerals and enzymes are, and so on. You can't eat a piece of chicken and automatically know how many calories are in each bite—not unless you've memorized the amount after endlessly double-checking Google.

You also don't talk about food in social situations the same way you talk about food when you're dieting. You don't go to a restaurant and order "50% protein, 30% carbs, 15% vitamins and 5% fats". You call food by what it is: Chicken. Rice. Beans. Carrots. In other words, the language of diet is not something we use in the real world.

That means scientific health explanations are not taught to us in a way that register intuitively or socially.

But what you did know innately was how foods *taste*. How they *feel*. You know that a lemonade on a summer's day will quench your thirst where as a hot chocolate in front of a fireplace makes you feel nice and cozy.

So what if you'd never learned any of that diet information? What if, instead, you had some kind of guide that showed you what to eat based on your *instincts* around how you wanted to feel, and that each time you followed this guide, you'd restore emotional and physical balance to your body? If you'd never heard any kind of scientific information about health in all of your years trying to get healthy, what would be the *clues* you could trust to guide you towards what to eat for your health?

Well, Mother Nature gives us three clues. And these three clues are cycles that influence our *environment* and our *body chemistry*.

Clue #1: Everything has a time and a place

Cycle 1: Seasons

The first *cycle* (aka "clue") around us that gives us insight to what foods to choose is the earth making one full orbit around the sun (aka "year"). Within one year, in most parts of the world, we have four seasons.

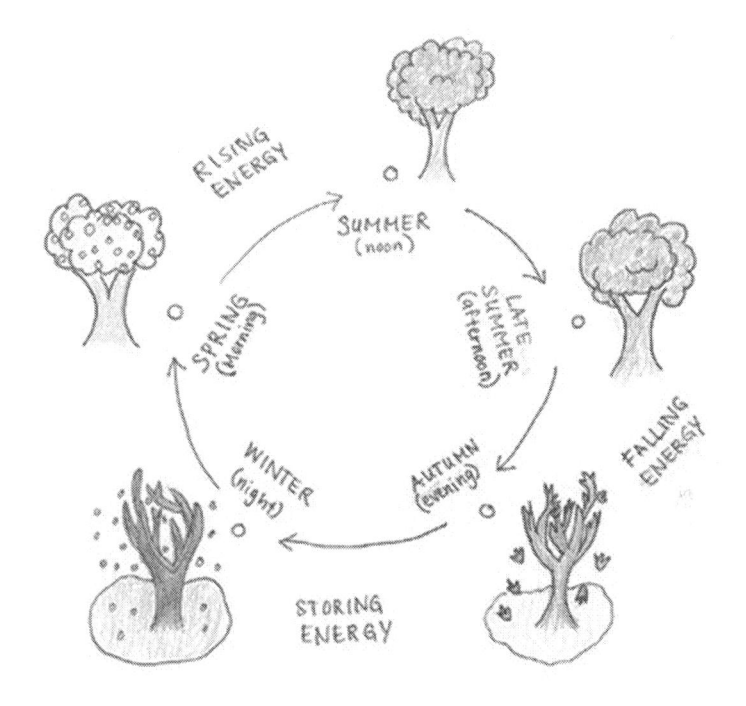

Seasonal cycle diagram: Spring (morning) – Rising Energy; Summer (noon); Late Summer (afternoon); Autumn (evening) – Falling Energy; Winter (night) – Storing Energy.

As the seasons change, our bodies require different kinds of support to help us acclimate to what is going on around us. When it's hot in summer, we need something cooling and hydrating to help us stay comfortable in the heat and to replenish the fluids our bodies lost from sweating. *Like a fresh, juicy watermelon.*

And in the cold winters, we need foods that are warming and grounding to help us have the energy we need to stay warm. *Like a nice warm carrot and ginger soup.*

The fruits and vegetables that grow in one climate cannot physically grow in another. They need certain elements, temperature, moisture, and conditions in order for the seed to sprout and the plants to grow.

If a fruit or vegetable cannot physically grow where you are during this time of year, is it the right *kind* of nutrition you need? Science suggests that it doesn't really matter *when* you eat foods, because you're going to put the same nutrition into your body, regardless of the timing. But holistic Eastern theories suggest only the foods that can survive in your climate are going to give you the *right kind of nutrition* for your body's needs at that time.

If nature offers us different foods during each of the seasons, does it make sense to aim for one perfect diet to have every day of the year? Alternatively, should we have a general format of eating where we *interchange the produce* as seasons change? Well, it doesn't make sense to search for that "perfect" diet you can have 365 days out of the year. Instead, it makes more sense to determine a *style* of eating based on food categories, and switch up the produce with each changing season. For example, maybe you decide to have fruit for breakfast. In summer, that could mean watermelon. And in winter, that could be an apple. You're still having fruit for breakfast, but you're interchanging the food according to what's best that time of year.

Have you ever had nutritionally dense foods but for some reason you didn't feel good after eating them? You'll probably notice for yourself that seasonal foods just *feel* better in your body. They're more energetically aligned to what we need where we are. For example, if I was in the tropics and had a mango while lounging around on a beach, that mango would probably feel so refreshing and scrumptious. But if I was at a ski lodge freezing my buns off and trying to warm up in front of a fire place, that same mango might not satisfy me the same way. It tastes the same and is giving my body the same nutrition, but the way I feel when I eat it is different. It won't feel as settling or nourishing as something like a warm root vegetable soup might feel.

I remember days when I tried having acai bowls or superfood smoothies in the middle of winter, and couldn't figure out why they felt so unappealing. Not so long before (during summer, of course), I had been enjoying them so much and would feel nourished and energized from them. As the seasons changed, I'd feel uncomfortable after consuming them. It's kind of like finding the perfect cashmere sweater. It's soft and warm and stylish. But wear it to the beach on a hot summer's day and you're one hot, sweaty, itchy mess.

I'm from Florida (known as the "Sunshine State"), an area that's hot most of the year. So in my case, I never really grew up with an understanding about seasons and variations in produce. The only thing I thought that was special about seasonal foods was that produce happened to taste best when they were at their peak.

Maybe you live in an area where you've experienced all four seasons for most of your life and have an intuitive understanding of this concept. Even in that case, many people don't ever reflect on how important it is to eat with the seasons and it certainly isn't highlighted when we are taught about nourishment.

Bottom line? There's a time and place for everything.

Have you been eating local, seasonal produce? Or, have you been importing a variety of produce and superfoods from distant locations?

If you're not sure what grows in your area, all you have to do is a Google search on what fruits and vegetables are in season that time of year. And if you happen to live in an area where there isn't a lot of fresh produce, it's okay to import from areas that are in a similar latitude or climate that matches where you are located.

Nature provides you with the best nutrition you can select to support your body as each season changes. This is the first clue to how to eat that we don't often hear from conventional diets.

Clue #2: You fluctuate with your own cycle

Cycle 2: Moon

The second clue we see in nature is the lunar cycle, which is when the moon makes one full rotation around the earth over the course of a month. Do women experience something health-related on a monthly basis too? *Of course... menstruation!* Are these connected? *Oh yes!*

In traditional health philosophies, it's often questioned that if the energy from the moon can have such an impact on the ability to move bodies of water in and out with the tides... *and* if the majority of our bodies are made up of fluids... then what kind of effect do you think the moon energy would have on our body fluids?

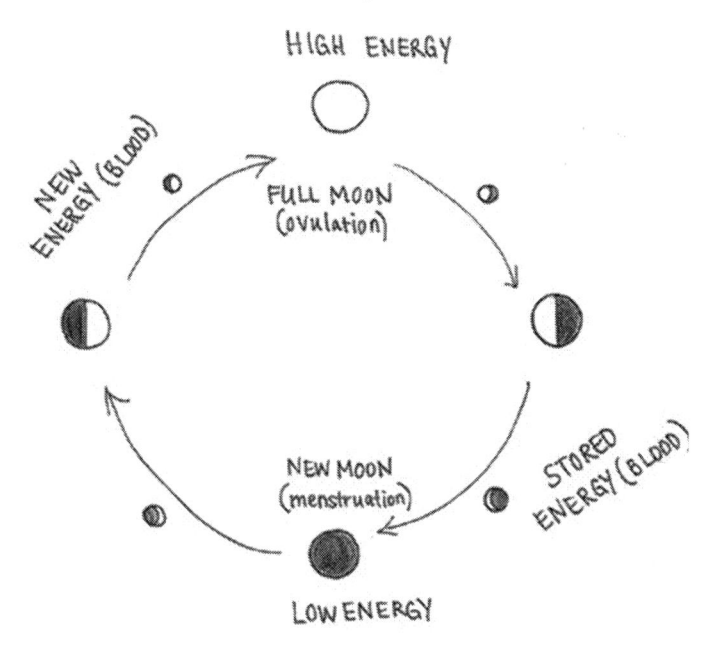

HIGH ENERGY

FULL MOON
(ovulation)

NEW ENERGY (BLOOD)

STORED ENERGY (BLOOD)

NEW MOON
(menstruation)

LOW ENERGY

The theory is that our menstrual cycles will begin along with the New Moon. This is when it's completely dark outside and there is no moonlight. It's a time for rest as our bodies are releasing all the blood stored in our uterus over the past month. From that point on up until the Full Moon, our bodies are building more energy and creating more blood to replenish all that has been lost. As we have more blood, our temperature starts to rise and we ovulate around the Full Moon, which is considered a time of high energy. Between Full Moon ovulation and New Moon when we menstruate, our bodies are continuing to accumulate blood to prepare the perfect environment for a fertilized egg—and if not, then that blood becomes expelled in the next period at New Moon.

What does this have to do with diet?

Well, there are a couple of ways this impacts our energy, appetite and body weight. For starters, most women are aware that their body weight fluctuates with their menstrual cycle. Typically, they feel a bit heavier during their periods, and lighter at other times during their cycle. If that's the case, then it doesn't really make sense for us to aim for a specific goal weight when we're trying to get healthy and rebalance our body weight. Instead, it makes more sense to target a weight *range* (of say, around 3-5 pounds) where we feel equally comfortable at the low and high ends.

Sometimes I meet women who beat themselves up over the "last five pounds", and I wonder if that weight is a natural part of their cycle. Why aim for one goal weight when it's guaranteed to fluctuate?

The second reason the menstrual cycle is important is because you have different energy levels and appetite throughout the course of it. It doesn't make sense to force yourself to eat all of your meals throughout the day if what you really need is a rest. It also doesn't make sense to restrict yourself when your body might need some extra energy.

Trust that the volume your body is craving is in accordance with what you need at that time. If you feel hungry and eat more than usual today, you might notice a week later you don't feel as hungry and eat less. It all balances out over the course of the cycle. It's okay to eat the volume that feels right to you. Cups, bowls and plates don't determine the right portion size. You'll know the right portion size when you eat.

Your hormones are directly connected to your weight balance. If you think there is something wrong with your hormone balance, consult with a functional nutritionist who can help you understand how to regulate your hormones through food and lifestyle. The more you know about yourself, the more ideas you'll have to help yourself create the balance you need.

Your energy, appetite and weight are going to change over the course of your cycle. This is clue #2 from nature.

Clue #3: Happiness comes from good sleep

Cycle 3: Night and Day

The third clue is the cycle of the sun rising and setting. This is when the earth makes one full rotation, which is the equivalent of a day or 24 hours.

When the sun rises, we rise. When the sun's down, we sleep. Pretty straight forward, but also one of the simplest forms of self-care that is taken for granted. When the sun rises, our body switches our body chemistry from melatonin (which helps us sleep) to serotonin (which helps us feel awake and alert). And when the sun sets at night, the opposite happens—our bodies convert from serotonin back to melatonin.

Serotonin affects three things:

- Awakeness
- Happiness

- Appetite control

Wait wait…hold on…Say what?! This *one* chemical in your body is like your natural happy drug that also tells you to stop eating when you're full. If you don't get adequate sleep—or if you're getting enough sleep but you're not sleeping when it's dark outside, for example, shift workers with irregular work schedules—you're increasing your chances of feeling exhausted, depressed, and unaware of when to stop eating.

Once, I had a manager who worked a 1-10pm shift. When I saw her about six months later after I had left the company, I was surprised to see that she had slimmed down and looked radiant. She was so perky, her skin was glowing, and her clothes fit better. She revealed to me that she had lost about 12 pounds. When I asked her what she had done, she said she'd done nothing different except her shift hours had changed to 9am-6pm. Before, she was going home and eating dinner after midnight. Since grocery stores weren't open around that time, she'd wind up getting some kind of processed meal from a convenience store. She'd sleep in the next morning until around 10am feeling completely groggy, and then start her day all over. On her new shift, she goes home at a "normal" hour and has more dinner options. She goes to bed before midnight and wakes up around 7am. She feels refreshed, her appetite decreased, and she's more productive at work.

Without forcing herself to count calories, join a gym, or any crazy dieting, she was effortlessly able to lose weight thanks to having a better flow to her lifestyle.

How tired are you?

Most people don't even realize how tired they are, because it's something they've become so used to. It's not like we have much opportunity to take an entire week to rest. Even if we do, it's usually to get over a cold or go on vacation where there's hardly time for restful sleep anyways.

To give you a better example, the weightiness you feel from poor circadian rhythms is kind of like jetlag. Your body feels heavier and you're in this dazed flux where your brain is "on" but your body hasn't quite caught up. It could mean you eat at odd hours during the day. You feel so much better once you've overcome jetlag and have adjusted to the same rhythms of the location you're in. Imagine having that jetlag—even on a mild level—on a daily basis.

You'll feel most refreshed when you are awake during the day and asleep at night. But if your circadian rhythms are off, then you can feel brain fog during the day, and exhausted at night, but unable to sleep since your brain feels switched on.

Have you ever gone to bed early—say, 10pm—and woken up feeling alert, but noticed it was only 5am? Some people sleep for the same seven hours going to bed at 2am, waking up at 9am, but feel groggy and weighed down when they get up. In Eastern theories, the peak time for our body to restore and repair is between the hours of 10pm and 2am. The more sleep you can get when it's dark out and wake up closer to the time the sun rises, the more likely you'll feel refreshed.

Why women won't sleep

I asked some women—corporate workers, entrepreneurs, stay-at-home moms, college students—why they felt uncomfortable *allowing* themselves to get more sleep. Here's what they said:

"I have a lot on my to-do list and going to sleep sounds *inefficient*."

"I have a demanding job where I like to get up at 5am to check my email and see what I have to do that day. Sleeping more makes me feel *irresponsible*."

"Sleeping is perceived as *lazy*."

"I feel like I'm *wasting* my life if I stay in bed. I can sleep when I'm dead."

"I need to do work and exercise. I feel *guilty* for choosing sleep instead."

I can see it now... We're at your funeral and your oldest child stands at the podium to say a eulogy.

"My mom was such a responsible, efficient, hardworking person who impressed us all by how much she never slept. Sure, she was also crabby, stole my donuts, and stopped listening to me every time we passed by a Starbucks when her nose caught a whiff of their addictive coffee. And sure, our deepest, heart-to-heart conversations was when she was actually sleep-walking. But you know what? Through all those tough times, my mom was just showing us true sportsmanship in her daily fight to not sleep. May she finally, *finally* rest in peace."

Tee hee! Couldn't resist!

All jokes aside, do you notice a pattern in these responses?

Sleeping makes us feel like we're not doing anything. And because we've grown up learning how to be responsible adults, "not doing anything" doesn't fit with our definition of responsible.

But hold up a second, overachiever. Your body *is* accomplishing something when you sleep. Your body is repairing muscles, regulating your hormones, creating appetite control, and rejuvenating your brain. It's really hard to maintain a healthy weight and curb wild cravings when you're not getting enough sleep. Let me repeat that: it's really, really, *really* hard to maintain a healthy weight and avoid wild cravings when you're not getting enough sleep.

If you're the kind of person who would rather stay up an extra hour to exhaust yourself at the gym because you don't want to miss out on an opportunity to lose weight, know that sleep can be a more effective strategy in helping you towards your health goals instead. If you're the kind of person who is practically a professional dieter because you've got your diet and exercise reps measured out precisely, but you never get sleep and you complain about cravings all the time… maybe you're putting your energy in the wrong areas.

Know that you can't be selectively healthy. If looking responsible to your family and coworkers is important to you, then shouldn't you be showing up every day 100% charged and ready to go? You know what? You're being lazy and irresponsible for *not* getting sleep or showing up as the most refreshed, recharged version of yourself. *There, I said it.*

If you want to show up in the world as the best version of yourself, then you have to show up with your batteries 100% charged.

Gaining the weight

Before we move on, I want to jump in here and comment on how I gained weight in the first place, because it's especially relevant to this topic.

The first 10-20 pounds I had been trying to lose back when I started Weight Watchers as a teenager were mostly due to just needing to figure out my eating habits and how to feed my body more nutrition. But the additional 20 pounds I put on when I went to school? That came on *really* fast. When I say fast, I mean between winter and spring breaks, which was the span of about two and a half months.

The issue in my case wasn't really one of those "freshman 15" scenarios, because I didn't accumulate the extra weight over the course of the school year. I only gained rapidly in winter time. Being from Florida, the Sunshine State, when I moved to Connecticut, it was my first time living in an area with cold, long, dark winters. My body went through a kind of shock from the environment.

All I wanted to do was stay in bed all the time because I felt so groggy. My eating habits, as you're fully aware (**cough* brownie binge*), were out of control. I couldn't figure out why I felt so down all the time, because on the surface, I was happy with the school and people around me. I didn't have a logical explanation for not feeling my best. It's like my body was a squirrel that went into hibernation. I was stocking up on my metaphorical nuts and was ready to pass out and wake up when the weather was better.

In my last year of boarding school in Connecticut, I used a "happy light" alarm clock, which is a light you can set to get gradually brighter anywhere from 5-90 minutes before you intend to wake up. It mimics the rising sun which helps your body convert from melatonin to serotonin. That means you feel refreshed by the time you're supposed to wake up. I didn't gain any weight in my final year at school with the help of this light.

Suffering through a cold dark winter and using the happy light was the first time I realized our bodies are directly affected by our environment, down to the chemical level. This is probably why I fell in love with all of these Eastern concepts I'm sharing with you now, because I'd already experienced firsthand just how much impact your environment has on your body.

Consistent pattern in the cycles

Going back to the cycles, given that nature provides us with these clues as to how to be healthy, there's one more crucial point you should know. All cycles follow the same flow pattern:

—> new building energy —> peak —> falling energy —> storing

Mother Nature is a cool mom. Every day, she's like, "Honey, listen to Mama. The sun is going down now so you better go to sleep." Every month, she sings, "Full moon's out, time to grab a lover and make me a grandma."

Every year, she goes, "Sugar pie, it's cold outside, so here are some root vegetables to keep you warm."

And you know what you've been doing? You've been going to bed whenever you feel like (or whenever you can, based on your chosen lifestyle), trying to stick to rigid regimes rather than allowing your body to fluctuate naturally, and eating foods out of season because you heard they are "nutritionally dense". And Mother Nature is like, "Ummm okay… you're sitting there complaining, not paying attention, and feeling horrible, when I've been giving you exactly what you need."

You are directly affected by your environment. You *cannot* escape it. You can't just turn the sun off when you feel like taking a nap, or turn it on in the middle of the night like a light switch. Nature governs this effect on our body chemistry.

Now, you can't escape it… but what you *can* do is support your body through these transitions if you want to feel your best. Go *with* the flow.

Thinking differently

After piecing together these elements, these cycles, a lightbulb went on in my head. Actually, it was more like the *sun* had turned on and I could finally see through the haze of diet advice and theories. I had all of this information swimming in my mind and excitement rushing through my veins like I had stumbled upon the holy grail of how to think about my diet. *Finally*, I knew what I was working *towards*. I wasn't working towards a life of restriction and muscle pain. I was working towards establishing a *flow* within my body. And I could use these concepts and clues from nature for guidance.

It awakened a curiosity in me that went beyond diet and exercise. I felt part of a bigger system and I had all the tools I needed both outside and within myself. All of the stereotypical advice—eat your veggies, get your sleep, drink your water—finally served a *deeper* purpose. *What if nature and my body know what they're doing, and all I have to do is go with the flow?* Maybe the whole point of "getting healthy" wasn't about "blastin' off dat fat", counting calories, or how many reps I could do at the gym. Maybe the whole point was to support the body in natural body rhythms.

I had always had all these tools to get healthy, but these concepts helped me understand *why* each one was important and *how* they all fit together. I realized that my responsibility to my body was about supporting the flow by living and eating in a way that harmonizes with flow patterns. *Wait… all I have to do is go with the flow?* Exactly so.

Go with the flow

If it's all about going with the flow, the first question I had to ask myself was: how had I *not* been going with the flow up until now? I mean, I thought I was being healthy by dieting and hitting the gym, but what if all of the tactics I'd been using were actually getting in the way of my body trying to do its thing?

Well, for starters, I had been trying to eat less—but I wasn't feeding myself a variety of nutrition. I cared more about what a nutritional label said than seasons and timing. I was exercising, but to the point of exhaustion and increased appetite. I didn't think anything other than diet and exercise (like sleep and body care) were important.

These were signs of how I was getting in my own way and disrupting flow.

What happens if you don't go with the flow?

Any disturbance to these flow paths create an imbalance. And your body tries to correct those imbalances with *cravings* or signals of what you need to restore balance.

Any time you refuse to eat when you're hungry, you're going against the flow. Any time you refuse to sleep when you're tired, you're creating an opportunity for an equal and opposite craving, such as sugar or caffeine or both. *Not* doing what your body needs sets you up for intense cravings and feeling worse about yourself.

It's time to go *with* the flow.

Cravings: a sign of imbalance

Like a see-saw that's overbalanced, when you are too low or too high on what you need in your body on one side, your cravings increase on the other side. Cravings exist as a way for your body to nudge you to restore flow. The more out of balance you are, the more intense the craving.

If you are exhausted from a long day and it's the middle of

the afternoon, do you think your body is going to crave something to help you bring your energy from negative back to positive quickly with a drink like coffee, or crave something healthy without a boost, like herbal tea? *Coffee, right?*

Are you more likely to crave ice cream after you've had something sweet, or after you've had something salty? *Salty, right?*

Are you more likely to crave alcohol to destress after a day at the office, or on a Sunday morning when you're chillin' on the sofa? *After a stressful day, right?*

What imbalances do you have in your life where your cravings are cluing you in?

What forms of self-care are unnecessary?

Once I understood how different health techniques were geared towards restoring balance, I wondered if I could be implementing some techniques that I didn't need, because I already *had* balance in that area. I had tried most of the self-care practices out there: journaling, meditation, and other spiritual stuff. Frankly, I was not a fan. However, I had convinced myself to keep going because I'd heard all of the health benefits, and thought maybe I'd wake up one day and discover some sort of bliss from being committed to a daily practice.

Ever since I started thinking more about what it means to be *in balance*, I realized I didn't have an imbalance in the areas where journaling and meditation can help most. I didn't wake up in the morning with too much on my mind. I didn't lose sleep because of a to-do list keeping me up. At last, I gave myself permission to stop these forms of self-care and I felt a whole lot better.

Speaking of identifying where I was putting energy in the wrong places, I also started doing less exercise after I saw a live sumo wrestling tournament. While watching two strong, massive sumo wrestlers push each other around the tournament ring, my Japanese friend told me that sumo wrestlers have a lifestyle pattern where they do intense workouts in the morning with heavy lifting and strengthening, have a large lunch, and then take a nap. After their nap, they repeat the process again: lots of exercise and training, a large dinner, and straight to bed.

It occurred to me that I had been following a similar pattern with my physical care—I would exercise to the point of exhaustion which left me so hungry that I'd eat larger portions than I probably needed. By the end of the day, I'd be so tired from the workout and full from the dinner that I'd head straight to bed. And the results I was getting from that way of living was that I was super strong and had a lot of stamina, but I also had a thick layer of fat over my muscles (the way sumo wrestlers do, though on a smaller scale). Maybe the way I was approaching exercise was actually designed to create a stronger, larger body?

If what I wanted was to look more like a slender ballerina, then maybe the answer was to do more stretching and toning exercises that were actually designed for that kind of body. Ballerinas look like ballerinas because they do, well, *ballet*. They don't look like ballerinas because they do high intensity interval training, spin classes and kickboxing. This sounds so obvious now that I'm sharing it here, but it's not something that occurred to me prior.

When I considered why, I realized there was a common piece of advice you've probably heard: you need to find *the exercise that works for you*. As a type A person, I thought that meant that I needed to find an exercise that matched my all-or-nothing personality type, so I wound up choosing intense exercises that made me feel like I was putting in effort. Once I changed the exercise to more calming movements like walking, stretching, and pilates a couple times a week, my body started to lean out in the way I had envisioned.

I couldn't believe that doing less was helping me reap more of what I wanted—less stress meant less appetite, less exhaustion meant more energy. I had more energy to do consistent calming exercises, and less appetite requiring portion control.

So between self-care techniques I didn't need as well as exercises that weren't designed for the body I had in mind, I realized how much I was getting in my own way towards feeling healthier. What about *you*? Consider your current lifestyle and where balance is already present for you, and where activities might be creating you more obstacles.

Let's reflect

Some of these concepts might be new to you, so let's take a moment to reflect on what to do next.

1. Everything in nature flows in cycles. Nature and your body know what they're doing. It's time to go with the flow.

2. Cravings are a sign of a disruption to flow. The more imbalance there is, the stronger the craving.

3. Health practices on all planes (mental, emotional and physical) are designed to rebalance your condition. Where is balance already present for you? Are any of your current health practices either unnecessary or creating more obstacles?

Shifting my relationship with my body

Once I'd explored and understood nature and cycles, I looked at my body differently. It was gradual, but I found it more challenging to look at food types as devils or angels that would add or take away fat from my body. Instead, food started to represent something so much more. I saw food as a way to connect with my environment, as something to be enjoyed—*celebrated*, even—at their seasonal peak. Food became a key tool to regulate my body's natural rhythms so I could feel and look my best.

I used to think of the fat on my body as something evil to get rid of, but now I saw that fat as a reflection of the imbalance in my day-to-day life—be it from my environment or my choices. Like a mirror reflecting back a truth.

Once I started thinking more about cycles, balance, and body rhythms, I was on a mission to solve two questions:

1. What changed in my lifestyle when I moved to Japan that influenced my effortless 10-pound weight loss?

2. What would I need to eat to restore balance in my natural body rhythms?

Let's explore these two questions in the next sections.

Part 3: Lifestyle Change

When I moved to Japan, I didn't actively make an effort to change my diet, yet my body started to change naturally thanks to the alterations that happened in my lifestyle. But what specifically were those changes? What other changes needed to happen to restore me to full health and balance?

A phrase I'd heard *all the time* but hadn't given much consideration is this: "I don't want to diet. I want a *lifestyle change*."

Let's explore what this really means.

Defining "lifestyle change"

Maybe you've heard people say, "I don't want to diet. I want a lifestyle change." Maybe you've said it yourself. I used to say this to myself constantly. Like, on a daily basis. Yet, I hadn't sat down and asked myself what it *meant*. What I desired was to wake up and suddenly have all the motivation and willpower I needed to reach my goals. Consistent gym-hitting. Easy "no-thank-yous" to any fun foods that would sabotage progress.

I thought I knew what I needed to do to reach my goal. And motivation and willpower were the two things I wanted to appear miraculously for those goals to happen. But... is that really what a lifestyle change *is*?

I researched this question with other women, including online followers, weight loss forums, Facebook groups, and more. The answers came swarming in and what I learned was both interesting and surprising.

One response in particular stood out: "A lifestyle change is not something to do temporarily so that I can get back into my normal life; I will live this way (*watching* and *counting* and keeping *control*) for the *rest of my life*."

This woman's thoughts illustrate the majority of responses I received. The common theme is that we believe the *only* way to get healthy is if we *discipline* ourselves by monitoring and tracking our actions. In order to make these changes stick, that discipline has to have a *permanence* in our lives. There's no going back to fun snacks. No funny business. *Strictness* is the answer.

Next, I asked the reasons why women felt they weren't able to reach their health goals. The top three answers were:

"I would if I had more *willpower*."

"I would if I had more *time*."

"I would if I never had to interact with *other people.*"

Now, there's one thing I notice about *all* of these answers on lifestyle and ability to get healthy that is really striking. Can you see it? These answers have nothing at all to do with food. *Nothing*! Yet the first thing we look up when we're trying to get healthy is a diet or exercise plan we can do in less than five minutes for less than $5.

Why are we looking for answers in diet and exercise when our biggest concerns have to do with lifestyle?

Healthy "lifestyle" or a lifestyle for health

Here's the wrong question we've been asking ourselves: does my health support my lifestyle?

When you lead with this question, your daily tasks become the main priority, and health becomes a chore. Your lifestyle choices, good or bad, become the central focus, and health becomes the afterthought. It becomes that tedious task that you know you need to do in addition to your crazy schedule. And you start generating excuses. You know you need sleep, but you need to finish that project. You know you need to hit the gym, but you're too tired. You know you need to eat healthily and make your own food, but it's a lot faster to order Uber Eats.

Let's look at how this might play out in some real-life scenarios. Perhaps you start searching for home workouts you can do in 20 minutes or less because you don't have time for a proper exercise session. Maybe you look up "healthy affordable recipes" because all of your cash has been spent on dry cleaning and gas to drive an hour to your job and that gym membership that you haven't had time to use. You could be looking up tips to help solve health issues *you have created* for yourself, like how to get rid of bloating or zits or under-eye circles or hangovers. You're constantly in "clean-up" mode to help reduce signs of poor health.

When you're caught up in a moment of feeling too tired to exercise or cook or do anything that would aid your self-care, the odds of you wanting to do it are minimal and you're left waking up the next day kicking yourself for not being "good" and promising yourself that today will be different. You believe the only way that you can make health happen is through willpower and discipline; willpower and discipline that you don't seem to possess. And so, you look *outside* yourself for *inspiration* and *motivation* to get yourself to do these healthy tasks.

Here's what we should be asking ourselves instead: does my *lifestyle* support my *health*?

When you reframe the question in this way, you're asking yourself if the way your life is set up is *creating* wellness or if it's causing you to *need* wellness. It means asking yourself if the big components in your life—your home, your job, your relationships, etc—are enabling you to have the time to sleep, access fresh, local seasonal foods, and be able to flow with nature's cycles.

When your lifestyle supports your health, wellness is a byproduct. You don't need willpower and discipline because your environment is set up in a way where it's *difficult* to feel stress, *difficult* to crave bad foods, and *difficult* and to make unhealthy choices.

I've observed this firsthand.

Lifestyle #1

See how my own lifestyle impacted my health and weight at different points in my journey:

When I was at my heaviest weight and at the worst of my binge-eating, I was living at boarding school where the campus was isolated from a nearby town. There were long, cold, dark winters that made me feel drained and cranky, and want to stuff my face with carbs. I was mentally and physically exhausted from having classes six days a week, ice hockey practice four times a week plus two games during winter season, and endless amounts of study work.

The amount of exercise that was built into my lifestyle was just the few minutes it took to walk between classes. So, maybe a total of 20 minutes of walking per day. Anything extra was intense workouts I did from ice hockey training sessions during that season, or extra gym time I made myself do in off-seasons in order to burn more calories.

The school dining hall was buffet style. Since there was a lot of variety and the menu changed on a daily basis, it was tempting to fill up my plate with more food than I probably needed, and it was also easy to go back for seconds if I happened to be chatting with friends for a long time. The cafeteria was the hangout place, so I felt compelled to be eating or nibbling on something even though most of the time I was there for conversation.

The students I lived with were also exhausted, not to mention homesick. The only places to get a change of environment and some fresh air off-campus was walking to the bakery (with amazing scones) just around the corner, or a Starbucks about 20 minutes away at the bottom of a hill.

So, let's piece this together: I had a demanding schedule, a lot of stress, peers who were feeling the same way. I was physically exhausted from sports activities, and the only places to have downtime were in a cafeteria where there's a buffet, a bakery, or a Starbucks.

Lifestyle #2

Now, compare that to when I was at my lowest weight. This is what my lifestyle looked like:

I was working at a job a 45-minute commute away via foot and public transport, of which I spent about 25 minutes walking. That meant I had 50 minutes of walking built into my daily schedule from my work commute. Plus, the nature of the job was doing projects that involved lots of moving around—not long hours of desk work. The location of my workplace was in a posh area that had a natural foods grocery store and organic cafes. The grocery store offered affordable organic lunch boxes for under $10, which I grabbed for lunch every day. If I had to stay later at work, I could always get some food at one of the organic cafes or pick up some easy-to-cook items at the grocery store on the way home.

The company itself was a design firm with great people, so even during challenging and demanding work times, I always felt surrounded by physical beauty and supportive friendship.

Piecing together this scenario, I had: exercise built into my commute/work, health grocery store/cafes/restaurants to stop by, colleagues who enjoyed their work, and an ability to go home at a decent hour and have a full night's sleep.

Do you see how the environmental set-up affected my ability to be healthy on a physical, emotional, and mental level?

Lifestyle #3

Let's check out one last example, for comparison purposes:

I changed jobs to a corporate office environment, as well as moving apartments to a location where my commute to work was a mere 8-minute walk. My body felt like it had changed a bit. I felt a little heavier and more sluggish compared to where I had been living and working before.

But instead of getting mad at myself (my previous "normal reaction" in the past, since I would have assumed I had done something to sabotage my health), all I had to do was step back and ask myself:

- *when* had I felt my body start to change, and
- *what* had changed in my lifestyle around that same time?

The answers were obvious: I was walking 16 minutes versus 50 minutes every day, sitting at a desk job instead of moving around, and didn't have the variety or quality of food options in the area I now worked, unlike the previous location.

With my new lifestyle, I recognized that I would have to go out of my way to cook healthier meals and to add exercise into my schedule if I wanted to live in the same balance I had before. There were also pros to my new lifestyle though. I was able to sleep more thanks to a better work shift and short commute. I had more time to cook healthy meals for myself. Sometimes, I could even walk home during lunch to have leftovers. I felt *alive* with the ability to set up my apartment in the exact way I wanted it. I felt *independent* and *excited* about my life on my terms. My body started to feel energized again with the couple tweaks I added. *No problemo.*

Does your lifestyle support your health?

In short, all this means you need to analyze your own lifestyle set-up to uncover where your choices are *helping* or *hurting* you, before you even embark on a diet or exercise plan.

Does your work challenge you in a way where you feel motivated, valued, and fueled for growth? Or does it make you so stressed out that you dread the idea of going, can't wait to escape to the break room for a coffee and donut, and are developing heart palpitations?

Are you in a relationship with someone who enjoys the same foods as you? Or is your partner stubborn to the point where you find yourself cooking foods only they like and wind up eating with them to avoid making more than one meal?

Do you have positive friendships that make you giggle and feel inspired? Or do you meet up with friends at a bar and the core topics are negative, so that one too many drinks leaves you feeling skeptical about life?

Does your work schedule and daily commute allow you adequate time to exercise how you want and get enough sleep? Or do you feel like you're getting up either ridiculously early or rushing out of work to make it to a workout class when you're *so* tired and just want to rest?

Are the closest places for you to buy food and groceries health food stores and farmers markets? Or are they gas stations and fast food restaurants?

Is your bedroom clean, your bedspread and pillow deliciously comfortable, and set up in a way where you can get your best quality sleep? Or do you leave the house in a rush without any intention of making your bed, letting in fresh air or even opening the blinds?

Does your home feel like a place where you can clear your mind and rest on all levels? Or is it a storage space of memories you don't want to relive?

If your biggest concern is that you need more willpower, ask yourself what's draining your energy or causing cravings and influencing you to get off track. If your biggest concern is not having time, explore how you can free up time in your schedule through re-assessing time management, removing unnecessary tasks, or even outsourcing. If your biggest concern is dining with other people, it's time to think more about how you communicate with others about the foods you want to eat, and why you find it important to eat in a way that might please others more than it pleases your body.

See how this works? Start with your lifestyle. *Does your lifestyle support your health?*

Set your health on auto

When I moved to Japan and my body and health started to change automatically, I realized that my *lifestyle set-up* and *environment*—my work, my commute, my food options, the cultural self-care—were making it easy for me to be healthy *without me having to put in any effort*. I *didn't have to think* about making time for a 50-minute gym workout, because walking 50 minutes a day was already built into my commute. I *didn't have to think* about whether or not my lunch was healthy, because the closest place to buy food at work was an organic grocery store that had lunch boxes. I *didn't have to think* about journaling for stress release, because I enjoyed the work I did as well as the people I worked with. I *didn't have to think* about having a secret cafe escape where I would munch on cookies and coffee, because for once, I wasn't overwhelmed by my responsibilities.

The point is: you want to set up your lifestyle in a way where you *don't have to think* about adding in extra effort to stay healthy.

Now, maybe you happen to be thinking, *Katheryn, it's great you were able to make changes and all, but I can't just leave my job and move my home and make new friends. That sounds like way too much change just to get healthy.*

True! It's a lot to consider. But... that's also kind of the point. You *do* have the ability to decide if you want to keep these major lifestyle components or if you want to change them. The point is that you recognize what aspects of your lifestyle set-up are holding you back from being healthy.

If something is that important to you to keep in your life, even though it might create obstacles to your health, then make a deliberate effort to do something to counterbalance its impact on your health, and do it with pride knowing that it's your decision to keep.

Think of it like an Olympic athlete. In order for her to continue to do intense training for hours each day towards her goal of winning a medal, she also needs to do just as many therapeutic treatments like sports massages, nutrition, acupuncture, passive heating, and so on, to counterbalance the stress that the training has on her body. That's the only way she can maximize her training performance day in and day out. And if she didn't train at all? She also wouldn't have to do as much physical therapy, because she isn't inducing stress on her body.

So that's where you need to start: thinking about lifestyle change and counterbalancing for yourself. If you have, for example, a stressful job that has deep meaning to you, then it's your duty to implement the self-care you need that will help you succeed. But if your job is stressful and has no meaning to you, then consider your next move and make sure you pick work that allows wellness to be integrated into your life.

Back when I was working at a company that was an 8-minute walk from my home, people constantly commented on how lucky I was to be living so close to work and having more time for myself. But that wasn't just by luck or accident—I set it up that way on purpose. Create *less* work for yourself around your busy schedule. Not more!

What is health?

This might appear to be going into something ridiculously basic, but stay with me. Before reading on, set this book down for a second and come up with your own answer to this question.

What is health?

Did you do it? Really. Pause for a second and think: *what is health*? If you're having trouble, think of it this way: *how do you know you're healthy?*

Once you have your answer, let me share with you some others I've heard:

"Health is when you just… *feel good*."

"It's when you feel *free*—no restrictions."

"Health is when I'm *stress-free*."

"I know I'm healthy when I'm *not sick*."

"Health is when I *feel happy*."

These are the common answers I hear whenever I ask women this question. If you analyze these answers, you'll notice that even though they all relate to health, each response is referring to something different.

Some are about **physical** health—*I know I'm healthy when I'm not sick*.

Some are about **mental** health—*health is when I'm stress-free*.

And some are about **emotional** health—*health is when I feel happy*.

When we're talking about "health", we're actually talking about three things: physical health, mental health, and emotional health. The dictionary definition of health is literally "soundness of mind, body and soul".

Health is feeling good

If there's one thing I realize now, it's that I only looked at "health" as a some kind of idea that would help me get fat off of my body. I wasn't learning about how my body actually worked or understanding how food affected me physically, mentally, and emotionally.

If you're reading this, I'm guessing you don't feel totally comfortable in your body either. You want to make changes to your physical health, but it's causing you a lot of mental and emotional stress. I'm sure you're clear on what physical health is—when your body is functioning optimally. Signs of poor physical health can be digestive issues, skin issues, aches and pains, low energy, etc.

But what's the difference between mental health and emotional health? Here's how I differentiate. Let's say you're overwhelmed with work. Your *mental* health is affected by the stress of all of the tasks that you have to complete. Your *emotional* health is affected by your boss telling you that you're a horrible worker who can't finish anything on time. So basically, *mental health* is based on your *mind,* *emotional health* is based on your *heart*, and *physical health* is based on your *body*.

This is interesting to me because most people trying to "get healthy" only think about one of the three: the physical. As a result, they take action only on the two factors they know could have a direct effect on physical health: diet and exercise. But the actions you take for your overall health have to encompass *all three*. Sometimes your diet might satisfy your physical needs, but not your emotional needs. Sometimes your exercise might clear your mind, but makes your body feel exhausted.

Feeling good is supposed to... *feel good.* That might sound obvious, but what it means is that the actions you take towards creating your health are supposed to be enjoyable. If the process doesn't feel good, even though it helps your body thrive, can that task truly be considered healthy?

Physical health is the absence of *dis-ease*

Another definition of health is "freedom from disease". When you're physically healthy, you don't have disease. You don't have dis-ease. Lack of dis-ease means our body has *ease*. In other words, in order for us to be healthy, we need our bodies to function *ease*-fully.

Ease. Easy, girlfriend. Make things *easier* for yourself.

We grow up in a society that honors hard work. But health isn't something you're supposed to have to work at. It's not about needing more discipline. Health works *and* feels best when you let go and let your body do what it's already designed to do.

What gets in the way of "ease"? Anything that makes it difficult for our bodies to process in an easy way can be described as "stress". Stress foods. Stress schedules. Stress relationships. All of this affects your body chemistry. Stress is when the body has to work harder to maintain its basic function. Whenever you choose a challenging job over sleep and emotional peace, you're challenging your body. The longer you leave yourself in an emotionally stressful situation, you're challenging your body. Whenever you work out to the point where you can't get up in the morning, you're challenging your body.

It's *easy* to become balanced with your weight when you have zero cravings, consistent energy levels, and a schedule that allows you to be healthy. Self-care isn't just about pampering *after* you're already exhausted. It's also about not putting yourself into situations that create a need for additional wellness; in other words, not placing yourself under undue stress.

Your job is to create the least amount of stress on your body as possible.

Alternatively, it's about knowing what to do to counterbalance stress when you do face those situations.

Think of yourself like a seed. You need certain elements in your life that will help you grow into the best version of yourself. Everything you've been doing has created the body you have right now. That includes all the diets and all the exercise you've done. If you're not happy with your body, something has to change. If you're already doing a ton of dieting and exercise, that doesn't mean that you have to do more. It just means that you have to find the right environment and combination that works with your body so you can thrive.

Your past actions have created your present. It follows that what you do today will create your future.

Lifestyle change or habit change?

There was one response I received from a woman sharing her thoughts on the definition of a lifestyle change that piqued my curiosity:

"Getting married, moving homes and changing jobs are lifestyle changes. If it's just eating a few different things in smaller portions, it's a **change of habits**."

This was probably the most interesting response I received. If you want to reach your health goals, do you believe you can do so in a way that makes you feel happy simply by tweaking your habits? Or, do you think it's necessary to make shifts in the bigger areas of your life?

Your environment triggers your habits.

If you change your lifestyle, then the habits you are trying to avoid typically get taken care of along with the lifestyle change. But if you're constantly triggered by your environment to have bad habits, you'll constantly have to monitor yourself to be healthy each time you're in that particular scenario.

Getting healthy is not supposed to be something you have to think about actively and only do when you have spare time. Health must be naturally built into the structure of your lifestyle and environmental set-up. So in this woman's example where she says she needs to change her habits to include smaller portions, a simpler task she could do is purchase smaller plates and utensils so she doesn't have to think actively about her portions each time she prepares a meal.

When I adjusted my lifestyle to how I wanted it to be, I was able to clearly see where it was helping me or not helping me be healthy. I could make habit changes to make up for what my lifestyle lacked. Trying to change my body didn't change my life. But changing my life? That changed my body.

So remember, your health and wellness are not just diet and exercise. It's about how *all* of the activities in your life influence your ability to be healthy.

Let's reflect

I'm sure that the core elements of your lifestyle are not the first things you think of when you're trying to change your body, but analyzing your lifestyle can set you up for success.

1. Reframe the question "Does my health support my lifestyle?" to "Does my *lifestyle* support my *health*?". Is your current lifestyle—where you live, where you work, with whom you interact, your hobbies—*creating* wellness, or causing you to *need* wellness?

2. To pinpoint a correlation between your lifestyle and your health, ask yourself two simple questions: *When* did your body start to change, and *what* changed in your lifestyle around the same time?

3. Health is about feeling good. It's about an absence of dis-ease. Your job is to make health come *easy* to you.

4. A habit change is not the same as a lifestyle change. Habit changes require constant awareness. A lifestyle change alters the environment you're in and removes the triggers that lead you to poor habits.

I'm sure by now you're dying to know what to eat for your diet. Now that we've talked about how the things *outside* your body can affect your health and habits, I will share with you how to think differently about what to put *inside* your body.

Part 4: Macrobiotics

With all that said, what are you supposed to eat? Well, now that we've covered how much your lifestyle impacts your choices, this next section is going to be on *how* to transition your diet.

For me, I had already lost 10 pounds simply by positioning myself in an environment where I was able to live more healthily without thinking about it. Yet, I still had a lot to learn about what to eat to re-establish these natural body rhythms and flow *within* my body.

What to eat

Have you ever felt like getting healthy is one big math problem? Counting, measuring, weighing... *talk about metrics*. I remember spending countless hours in the grocery store looking at nutrition labels and trying to figure out which option to pick. *Should I pick the one with lower fat but higher sugar, or higher fiber but more calories? But wait... this other one over here has a high protein content, and I heard that's super important... Or actually, maybe I'll go with the one that's low carb?*

I wanted to make sure that I was choosing the absolute best option, but it was so exhausting to figure out which one it was. How was I supposed to make the best decision for myself without overanalyzing every morsel that went into my mouth?

Understanding macrobiotics

In Part 1, I mentioned stumbling upon books about a concept called "macrobiotics". This is what helped me have an understanding of what kind of diet I needed to rebalance my body, mind, and natural rhythms. Here is a basic overview of the concept:

In nature, everything is made up of energy described as having "yin" or "yang" characteristics.

Yin energy describes foods that grows up and out, like leafy greens which grow in an upwards direction, and fruits which grow on taller plants like trees. Yin represents foods that make us *feel* uplifted, so in addition to these whole foods, it also includes refined sugars and refined grains. When eaten in balance, you'll feel awake, alert, and light in your body. In excess, you'll experience a high followed by a crash.

Yang energy represents the opposite: foods that have centripetal energy that moves inwards and downwards. You can visually see this in foods like root vegetables which grow down into the ground and become pointed towards the ends (such as carrots, daikon). Animal products are also considered yang as they are concentrations of the nutrition consumed by the animal. When you have foods with more yang properties, you feel warm and relaxed. In excess, you can feel lethargic.

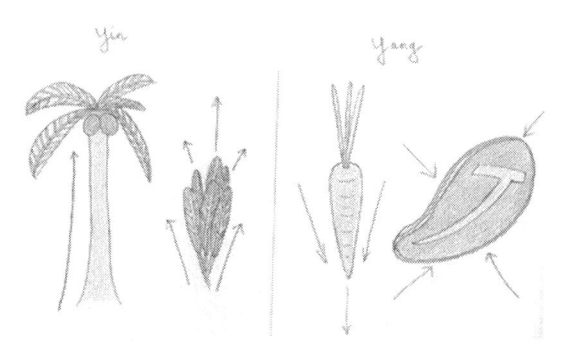

Macrobiotics is the *philosophy* of eating a variety of foods that give you a good balance between yin and yang. Ideally, within the spectrum of foods from yin to yang, rather than eating a combination of foods at the opposite ends of the chart, which have a polarizing effect on the energy of your body, you'll want to focus more on the moderate foods towards the center as these have a better yin and yang balance within themselves, and are less stressful on your digestive system.

Using this concept, *whole grains* are considered to be the most energetically balanced, and you can create a balanced meal by supplementing them with leafy greens, round vegetables, root vegetables, and beans.

What is a balanced meal?

In my survey, I asked the women participating what they thought a *balanced meal* is. Here are some of the answers I received:

"25% meat, 25% carbs, and 50% veggies."

"A balanced meal is a variety of color on my plate."

"It depends on your circumstances like age, diseases, etc. I have allergies so a balanced meal to someone else could be a trip to the ER for me."

"A balanced meal is a glass of wine in each hand."

I would say the most common answer I hear is the first one—that a balanced meal is considered some kind of ratio between proteins, carbs, and vegetables.

In macrobiotics, a balanced meal is a variety of foods that are energetically balanced between yin and yang. The foods you select depend on your climate, environment, age, sex, activity level, and personal needs. For example, the general makeup of a plate would be a combination of whole grains, root vegetables, round vegetables, leafy greens, and beans (or light animal protein), although the actual ingredients you choose would depend on what is offered in your area during the season.

What's cool about this concept is that you're seeing a spectrum of nutritional property from one end of the chart to the other.

Yin	**Yang**
wet	dry
vitamins	minerals
fats	proteins
sweet	salty
digests quickly	digests slowly

As you can see, by eating a bit of everything from this chart over the spectrum of foods, you would consume a wide variety of nutrition from one end of the range to the other. You also create *emotional* balance within your body. Technically, all of the answers that the women shared (except for the wine in each hand!) would be accurate. So to reiterate, think of having a bit of each of these: whole grains, leafy greens, round vegetables, root vegetables, and beans; those foods in the central area on the chart.

Think from day to night

Now that we have established what a balanced meal is, let's explore what to eat over the course of a day. We need to eat in a certain way that gives us the kind of energy we need at the right times of the day. Here's the thought process:

Morning (Spring)

Morning is a lot like springtime—a symbol of new beginnings, and an opportunity to be "out with the old, in with the new".

You've spent all night resting so your body is ready to get rid of wastes. The morning is a great time to have a bowel movement. Also, since you haven't been hydrating your body all throughout the night while sleeping, it's especially important to start your day with some water (especially lemon water) to hydrate your body and stimulate your digestive system.

Keywords: wake up; detox; out with the old, in with the new; hydration; vitamins.

Foods: fruits, porridge (oatmeal, rice), green vegetables, soups.

In the morning, since the aim is to hydrate the body, you'll want to avoid dry foods and dehydrating liquids. For example, if you have a piece of toast with a coffee, you've essentially fed yourself foods where the water has been baked out, and a beverage that is dehydrating. If you want to have bread and coffee, then consider steaming the bread, or adding in some soup or fruit to make up for the lack of water content.

It's okay to wait until you are hungry to eat. In Eastern health, the metabolism is described as a "digestive fire". When you eat when you're not hungry, it's like trying to put a bunch of logs into a fireplace before lighting a match. On the other hand, having a feeling of hunger is like having a fire started in the fireplace before you add the logs—the fire is more effective at consuming the wood.

For me, I tend to feel hungry as soon as I have a bowel movement. Some days, that's within 30 minutes of waking up. Other days, it's not for a couple of hours. If you're in a situation where you have to go to work and have time constraints to have breakfast, one thing you can consider is to have a consistent breakfast at the same time every day, which "trains" your body to be ready to eat at the same time on a daily basis.

Midday (Summer)

Midday is considered to be the peak of your metabolism and of rising energy. To put it in other words, it's where your digestive fire is at its strongest point. This is a good time to have a variety of everything, from raw foods to cooked foods to even fried food and animal products.

One pitfall some people run into is having a lunch that is too large and salty. This typically happens if you're too hungry come lunchtime and wind up going straight for that meatball and cheese sub. The more heavy yang foods you have, the more likely you'll find yourself having that afternoon slump while your body is working hard to digest.

Keywords: digestive peak, high energy, variety

Afternoon (Fall)

The afternoon is a great time to take a break and regroup. It's when your body is having a turning point between rising energy and falling energy. Some people worry about feeling a need for an afternoon pick-me-up, but in Eastern health this is a good time for a rest. I mean, you've likely been running around all day with work or chores, right?

The snacks you can have should be pleasantly uplifting, but not too strong. Consider naturally sweet round and root vegetables, like pumpkin and sweet potato. Warm fruits like a cooked apple and also nuts are great options. I loved having vegan macrobiotic tarts, like mixed nuts, pumpkin, or apple.

Keywords: rest time, regroup, naturally sweet vegetables, cooked fruits

Evening (Winter)

The evening time is when you want to think about having foods that will warm and relax your body in preparation for restorative sleep. Think more root vegetables, soups, stews, whole grains, beans and protein.

Since the aim in the evening is to create relaxation and warmth, you'll likely find it more pleasant to have cooked foods over raw ones. In Eastern health, raw foods (especially juices, smoothies, and salads) are considered uplifting and cooling to the body, which isn't the kind of energy alignment we're looking for in the evening. Experiment a bit and see if having warmer, cooked foods improves your sleep.

Keywords: relaxation, warmth, repair, protein, sleep

Unbalanced energies

Now that you have an overview of the theory behind how to eat in a way that restores physical and emotional balance, what happens if you eat in an unbalanced way?

Eating foods mostly towards the ends of the chart, either extreme yin or extreme yang, make you feel stronger reactions in your body both physically and emotionally.

Excess yin, like refined sugars and caffeine, can leave you feeling wired. You experience a sudden energy lift and likely a crash later on in the day. The more you have of foods in this area, the higher you'll feel when on a high—but the lower you'll feel when in a low. The more strongly you feel a low, the more strongly you'll crave another high. The emotional reaction you can feel from excessive yin foods is stress in the form of anxiety. You've given yourself uplifting energy but to the point where you're feeling a bit over-stimulated.

Now, if you have too many foods on the yang side of the chart, the opposite occurs where you might feel sluggish. Eating foods like heavy animal protein and cured meats with excessive salt in too great a quantity can take longer to digest, so you're more likely to feel weighed down. The emotional reaction you may feel from excessive yang foods is stress and depression. This is when your body feels heavy, you feel sad, and you lack energy or positivity to get through your day.

I hear some people say that they suffer from anxiety and depression. This means they're experiencing both ends of the scale, a polarized feeling and roller coaster of emotions where one moment they have fleeting emotions, the next they feel like gravity has pulled them down.

Yin or yang?

If you're not totally sure how a food will make you feel, ask yourself this question: If you gave this food to a 5-year-old, what kind of energy would that kid have?

If you give a kid a candy bar (yin), she'd probably be bouncing off the walls with hyper energy. On the other hand, if you give her a steak (yang), she'll probably be so tired that she'd fall asleep at the dinner table. Foods react in your body the same way they react in kids. We might feel it more mildly compared to children, or we might have gotten so used to ignoring how we feel that we don't relate it back to the food. Regardless, know that your body experiences the same reaction.

When I started thinking about foods in this way, I no longer felt like foods fell into categories of "good" or "bad". It seemed like everything was on the same plane but had a different level of stress reaction for the body.

What does your current diet reveal?

Let's do an exercise. On a separate piece of paper, write down all of the meals that you had, yesterday. If you can't remember or if you feel like yesterday was a particularly odd day where you ate foods that don't represent your typical eating habits, then write down what you typically have on a given weekday.

Then, next to each meal, write down all of the base ingredients. For example, if you had pancakes for breakfast, then write down refined white flour, eggs, and milk. You don't need to get overly detailed with condiments and spices—just the core ingredients will do. Here's an example:

Meal	Ingredients
Bagel with butter; milk tea with sugar	Refined white flour, caffeine, dairy, refined white sugar
Turkey and cheese sandwich (white bread); yogurt	Refined white flour, dairy, turkey
Chocolate chip cookie, iced latte	Refined white flour, dairy, refined white sugar, caffeine
Spaghetti with meatballs and cheese	Refined white flour, dairy, beef

Got yours down? Now, place a circle on each ingredient you've had on the chart.

Using the ingredients from the table above, see the example below. Notice the circles stacked on certain ingredients:

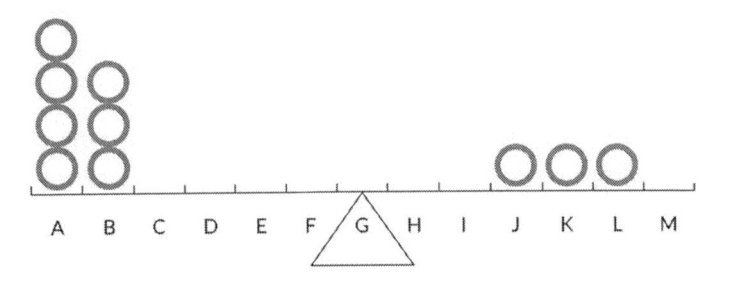

You can see that the foods I had been eating are further to the ends of the chart, which means they are more stressful for the body to process. I could sense this in my body both physically and emotionally. You'll also notice that no foods were eaten from the center area of the chart, which is considered the "healing" zone with better nutritional variety as well as ease on the digestive system.

Use this blank one for your exercise:

Yin Yang Balance Scale

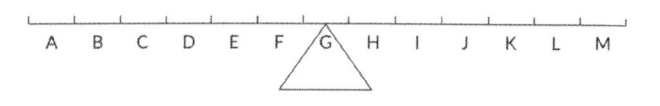

A   B   C   D   E   F   G   H   I   J   K   L   M

A	Refined Sugar, Caffeine (coffee, black tea, energy drinks etc.), Alcohol
B	Refined Grains (white flour/bread, white rice etc.), Fruit Juices, Soft dairy (milk, butter, yogurt etc.)
C	Tropical Fruits (bananas, mango, etc.), Nightshades (tomatoes, eggplant, peppers, white potatoes)
D	Temperate Fruits (fruits that grow in areas with all four seasons, like apples)
E	Leafy Greens
F	Round Vegetables (onions, turnips, pumpkin, cabbage, etc.)
G	Whole Grains (brown rice, whole wheat, barley, millet, oats, rye, etc.)
H	Root Vegetables (carrots, burdock, sweet potato, etc.)
I	Fish, Seafood
J	Poultry (chicken, duck)
K	Pork, Lamb, Cheese
L	Beef, Eggs
M	Cured Meats (bacon, ham, prosciutto etc.)

What does this exercise reveal to you? You'll see in the example that most of the foods fall on the sides of the chart, with hardly any circles of foods closer to the center.

Have you been eating a variety of foods across the chart?

Do you notice that you're eating more foods towards the outsides of the chart and fewer around the middle? Are you eating mostly foods from one side more than from the other?

Now, keeping in mind that excess yin foods can make us feel anxious or high followed by a crash, and also keeping in mind that yang foods in excess can make us feel heavy, tired, and depressed, do you notice a correlation between the foods you've been eating and how you feel?

Some people who write out the ingredients they've been having find that they're doing great with their diets, so it gives them peace of mind to recognize that they're doing well. Other people do this and discover how many gaps there are in their diets.

Use this exercise to help you gauge your starting point and see where you're missing out on key nutrients.

When I first tried food journaling (which made me feel even guiltier since I had to admit to myself what I had been eating), I *thought* I had variety in my diet.

For breakfast, I'd have a bagel.

For lunch, I'd have a sandwich.

And for dinner, I'd have spaghetti.

But if you break them down into their ingredients, I've basically had refined white flour, three times a day.

What do these foods have in common: muffins, french toast, danish, cupcake, quiche, pancake, crepe, scone? Answer:

They are all made out of the same ingredients in different proportions. For some reason, we think that having eggs with toast is a decent breakfast, but french toast is naughty. Essentially, they're the same thing! We think that muffins are a breakfast item, but cupcakes are a celebratory treat. They're also pretty much the same ingredients.

Don't let your perception of food items get in the way of the facts—the facts being the ingredients you put into your body.

Let's reflect

I'm excited to be able to share an overview of macrobiotics with you, because most people who learn about it are searching for healing through whole foods. If you're looking to change your weight, you might not be searching for "healing", but to me, these concepts are a basic template anyone can use to restore balance, regardless of their starting point.

1. Macrobiotics is a philosophy of eating seasonal foods in a balance between yin and yang. When you eat a variety of seasonal foods, you're providing your body with a wide spectrum of nutrition, and an opportunity to find emotional balance.

2. Think about the flow of the day from morning to night as though it is a cycle of seasons. You need a different kind of energy and support at different times during the day. It's not wrong to eat against the suggested pattern in the future when you feel your best, but in the beginning this method can help you in re-establishing flow.

3. The foods at the ends of the macrobiotics chart are considered to be more stressful on the body. The more you have of these foods, the more likely you are to create strong cravings.

4. Start with your own self-evaluation. You can do this by looking at the core ingredients you eat throughout the day and see if there is a correlation between what you eat and how you feel.

Next, we are going to talk about how you can transition your diet, as well as common pitfalls most dieters encounter when trying to get healthy.

Part 5: Transitioning Your Diet

Now that you have an understanding of what it means to be in balance, and have also gauged how your current diet is making you feel, let's delve a bit more into how you can transition your diet and why it doesn't have to be so hard.

For me, I could grasp why this yin and yang theory made sense and had a strong urge to follow it. All of this balance stuff sounded amazing, but I still had two problems:

1. Healthy food didn't taste great, or had no flavor at all.

2. I still had intense sugar cravings. And caffeine cravings. And salty food cravings.

In other words, I understood what I had to change, but my body wasn't receptive nor making it easy.

Wholegrain bread tasted like cardboard, oatmeal tasted like *wet, soggy* cardboard, raw superfood chocolate balls tasted like hardened balls of cough syrup, green juices tasted like lemon-scented kitchen counter cleaner. Well, I haven't ever eaten cardboard and I don't tend to consume cleaning solutions, but in my imagination, that's what they tasted like.

And it turns out I'm not the only one who had an aversion to healthy foods. Here's what other women have said about their health food experiences:

"Quinoa smelled like sweaty gym socks."

"Date nut bar tasted like rubber tires."

"Green smoothies tasted like that seaweed trash gunk that collects on the beach."

"Rye toast tasted like tree bark."

The struggle is real.

But I was beyond convinced by the concepts that these whole, seasonal foods were what I needed in order to establish flow. I believed that these healthy foods *must* have an appealing taste to people, because they were what nature intended for us to enjoy. How was I going to get used to eating them *and* overcome my cravings at the same time?

A common pitfall

Most people I see who go on diets typically start with trying to eliminate the foods on the extreme yin and extreme yang ends of the chart. In other words, they start with trying to cut out sugar, caffeine, refined flours, cured meats, etc. This makes logical sense; if these foods are the most polarizing, surely trying to cut them out would put the least amount of stress on the body and therefore help you reach your health goals faster.

The problem in doing this is those moments when we are most tempted by high stress foods; the decision to eat those foods happen in response to cravings. If you crave a chocolate chip cookie, then stopping yourself from having one doesn't get rid of the craving. You might find that you can discipline yourself for a short time, but the second you're in a situation where you're exposed to those foods again, it's impossible to "get back on the wagon" after a bit of temptation.

Starting with cutting out what you crave the most is probably not the best idea, because you haven't addressed the root cause of the craving. You're just prolonging the craving, letting it fester and fester into a binge-fest-gone-wild. The concept of a diet is easy in theory. You just eat one healthy food over a non-healthy food. Pretty straight forward. But it's not that easy when we have urges to respond to cravings.

Instead, consider trying to increase the amount of nutritionally and energetically balanced foods from the center of the chart into your diet. This includes alternative sweeteners, coffee replacements, plant-based milks, etc. This will help your body start to learn about less stressful ingredients and add a sense of "calm" to your emotions. It's a lot easier to experiment with weaning yourself off of high-stress foods after you've explored the alternatives.

You don't have to do anything super drastic when you're starting out. Back when I had a bagel, sandwich and pasta, instead of completely altering my diet, I could have easily had my normal bagel for breakfast, a sandwich made with rye bread, and pasta made out of brown rice, which would have enabled me to eat what felt comfortable while still introducing my body to different kinds of nutrition.

For most people, they don't care about what's in their basic breakfasts, lunches, and dinners as much as they do about their first cup of coffee or afternoon donut fix. If that's the case with you, start by making your basic meals awesome instead of cutting the foods you're emotionally attached to the most.

Also, keep in mind that the only way to train your body to crave healthier foods is to reduce the source of stress and exhaustion in the first place. Don't cut out everything you know to be unhealthy for you and expect your body not to crave them without first eliminating the stress that gives you the cravings in the first place. In other words, if your cravings are a direct result of trying to escape your office in the afternoon because of the toxic work environment, then don't expect the cravings to go away completely until that situation has changed. That's where analyzing your lifestyle (like we did earlier in this book) comes in handy.

At the end of the day, in order to harmonize with nature and these rhythms, the first step is to eat more local, seasonal foods in their whole form.

Being nice, for once

I already knew from countless diets that forcing any kind of method of eating onto myself would not be the right approach. It dawned on me that there's one thing I hadn't tried yet. And that was to be nice to myself.

"Being nice" meant two things:

1. Experimenting with feeding my body more nutritionally dense foods, but only as much as I felt comfortable with.

2. Honoring my cravings if I was dying to have something not-so-healthy, with a rule to enjoy every bite.

This "being nice" thing gave me the chance to explore ways of supporting my body that I hadn't actively tried before, while also not putting myself down when old habits popped up. Feeling guilty was *not* allowed.

Why did this work? Well, for starters, I recognized *finally* that the wild cravings and bad feelings I had were all imbalances that I had created for myself based on my past lifestyle and food choices. In other words, I knew that these feelings were a result of my own actions, and not because my body "hated me". I'm responsible for how I want to feel, which means everything I had done up until that point had created the body I had—cravings, low energy, excess weight included. I needed to acknowledge and honor that.

When I'd tried diets in the past, I kept wondering if I would be happy if I mastered the art of sticking to it and achieved my weight goals. I didn't feel confident about that. But with the method I used to get to where I am now, the concept is the same today as it was in the beginning: I engage with life when I feel like it but also put forth my best effort when I do have options. This has made the biggest difference, because it's not like I achieved my weight goal and then all of a sudden had to figure out how to adjust my diet for maintenance. I still approach my daily eating pattern in the same way I did back on day one. Scones were never off limits when I started my transition; they still aren't off limits now.

Keyword: *transition*

If you wanted to lose weight and transform your body by, well, *yesterday*, then the idea of only putting in 20% effort when you could be putting in 100% to get results faster might seem like a waste of time. The point of transitioning is to establish a connection with foods, to understand how you feel with them, and to sense the changes that are happening in your body.

When you go in 100%, you don't get a chance to recognize what parts of the new healthy lifestyle you actually enjoy, because the little bits that aren't working can overshadow the entire experience and lead to self-sabotage. Going at it gradually helps us become more conscious about what's working and what's not.

I was living in a small vintage town with narrow streets and bustling businesses stacked on top of one another. Nearby my apartment, there was a rice shop that sold a dozen different kinds of rice from all over Japan. But what I found really cool about this place is that you could request for them to shave off a percentage of bran from the rice. Instead of only having two options—brown rice or white—I could get 1/8 brown rice, 1/4 brown rice, 1/2 brown rice, 3/4 brown rice, or 100% brown rice.

Ding! The lightbulb went on.

It was the first time I'd discovered transitioning as an option. Before, I had assumed that my only options were either to enjoy refined grains with guilt, or to eat whole grains and feel unsatisfied.

All it took was having 1/8 brown rice to make me feel excited about taking a step towards better health without completely compromising my experience with taste or texture. The 1/8 brown rice tasted like white rice, but with a naughty secret. I felt like I was tricking myself into getting healthy and this trickery was what built a fun relationship with food. Once I got used to 1/8, I moved up to 1/4, and so on until I thoroughly enjoyed having 100% brown rice.

Jumping from white rice to brown rice is like trying to climb a mountain before you do a trail hike. (I've done that... I climbed Mount Fuji before knowing what it meant to go hiking. *Oops!*) From experience, let me tell you that you don't appreciate how enjoyable the climb could be because your body hasn't been prepared to handle an experience of that nature. You're not conditioned and it just feels hard.

It's the same with transitioning your diet. You need to recognize that your body isn't used to these new healthy foods you're eating, and needs some time to adjust. The end goal is truly fulfilling if done in the right way. So I went in with full trust that brown rice was going to be something I *could* crave down the line, while also fully acknowledging that my body wasn't in a position to tune into it without some practice. It's *okay* to transition. If you try to leap, you might find yourself in a place that's a bit too far out of your comfort zone.

Start out gradually

Have you ever heard someone say that if you're craving sweets (like chocolate cake) to have a piece of fruit (like an apple) instead?

Ha! Like that's ever worked.

I don't even know how we can compare a piece of chocolate cake and an apple—they're *totally* different. Sure, they're both "sweet", technically. But it's a different *kind* of sweet. The cake is more of a soft sweetness that fills your mouth with a warm comfort. The apple is more of a sharp, tart taste. They have different textures. They have different consistencies. They *feel* different in your body.

When you're craving a piece of chocolate cake, sometimes you're not just craving the flavor. You're craving the *experience* you have with the cake, which is only satisfied by having that texture and feeling in your body.

When you're starting out, you don't have to take a leap

from chocolate cake to an apple. Instead, maybe you start by using healthier ingredients in the cake. Maybe you make it a vegan chocolate cake. Maybe you try using maple syrup as a sweetener instead of refined sugar. Maybe you try using a different kind of flour instead of refined wheat flour.

What'll happen is you'll start to discover healthier versions of that cake that still satisfy the experience you were craving. And since the ingredients are less stressful on your body, it's easier to wean off the cake in the future, if that's what you want to do.

Start where you are

What you need right now might not be what you need in the future, and vice versa. When I was at my heaviest weight, eating a salad didn't feel good. It made me feel like the vinaigrette was burning my esophagus. I felt hungry and always went searching for something else that had more flavor and created more fullness. At the stage I was at, it was a lot easier to start off with cooked veggies in stronger flavorings like garlic or curries.

Maybe you don't need to eat salads and smoothies right now—maybe starting with cooked veggies is where you're at. It will evolve. And even if you find something that feels great in the future, your body will change again as you age, have babies, etc. The point is to develop trust with your body and with nature. Follow the clues as you continue to change as well.

Think of it like an experiment... not a definitive change. Maybe what you think you need isn't what you need right now. When you think of making changes as being permanent, there is a lot of anxiety about making that change. But when you do an *experiment*, you tell yourself it's temporary, give the concept a chance, and then decide at the end if you want to keep it or not (or keep bits of it).

The best part is that *you* can be the judge of whether or not the experiment was a success.

The effects of being nice

I was surprised at how much I was discovering about myself and about food once my approached changed. Food became more interesting, my preferences became more clear, and my body was responding in a positive way. Your personal journey will be unique, but here's my experience to give you an idea of what could happen.

For starters, my bond with food became deeper. I remember slicing an organic carrot and there was this sweet, unusual aroma. *Is that a carrot!?* I started sniffing the carrot the way you'd "accidentally" sniff nail polish remover a few times. When I gave the carrot my full attention, I felt like I was experiencing it for the first time. I hadn't know before what a carrot tasted like raw, steamed, boiled, grilled, fried, or baked without any kind of sauce or seasoning. The true flavor of the carrot had always been masked by something else.

I also realized which foods I didn't like but was eating because I thought they'd make me healthy. It dawned on me that I'd never really liked chicken breast, but I was eating it regularly thinking it was a great source of protein and good for weight loss. I also discovered that I didn't like a lot of raw foods, like raw salads, especially with vinaigrettes. And I really hated protein bars. Bleh. 'Nuff said.

Once I started cutting out the foods that I didn't like, I started giving myself permission to have more of the healthy options that I do like. I got caught up in a love affair with kabocha (a kind of squash), which previously I would have never tried because I thought it was too starchy, which is "bad" for dieting. I loved kabocha so much that it instantly replaced my desserts. It's obviously a lot better to have a natural vegetable as a dessert instead of processed sugars, so this was a win-win step.

I also gave myself permission to eat things like organic corn, another natural food I thought was devilish. I noticed that the more naturally sweet plant-based foods I had in my main meals, the less I craved desserts.

I started getting comfortable with eating pasta. I tried ones made out of whole grains, from whole wheat to brown rice to amaranth and more. It was fun to eat and I knew I was feeding myself new kinds of nutrition.

I used to think that I needed to eat more protein and fewer carbs if I wanted to lose weight, and my interpretation of that advice meant to eat more animal products like chicken breast, and fewer grains and starchy foods. But eating a diet heavy in animal protein meant I was consuming foods that took a long time to digest, without any fiber or hydration from more veggies to help my body process the foods. *TMI alert!* Back when I was at my highest weight, I was incredibly constipated. I only went number two about two to three times per week. And when I did, it was ridiculously painful because my stools were so large and dry. When I started eating more whole grains and root vegetables and fewer animal products, my bowel movements increased from twice a week to once per day. Cue the choir: Hallelujah!

Weight loss is a byproduct of a smoothly functioning system in balance. Don't try to reinvent the wheel when you're changing your diet. You don't have to start off with a smoothie made with 50 superfoods. It's okay to start with just one apple. What do you like about it? What do you dislike? Out of the countless varieties and colors, which do you enjoy most? Least? Do you like it raw, cooked, baked? Do you like it with spices? The questions and varieties are vast, so it's time to start putting your taste buds to work.

Intuition is BS in the beginning

When I was dieting, I remember being intrigued by the concept of "intuitive eating". I read books that would say that all you had to do to be healthy is to listen to your body, chew well, and have "awareness" for everything that goes into your mouth. I liked how that sounded. It seemed so nice to be able to have a relationship with my body where I could just sense what it needed and respond accordingly to its requests. But there were a couple problems with this concept.

The first was that there is no clear path to understanding how long it takes to create a hot, sexy body through intuitive eating. I wanted to lose weight, like, *yesterday*. If I listened to my body, would I transform quickly? Would it take months? Years? How could I trust my body to change when every diet plan with a definitive outcome hadn't worked? How could I trust my body to change for the better when all I craved were cookies, which I was *pretty* certain wasn't the healthy choice to follow?

And the second problem was that I couldn't have awareness or honor my intuition *all* of the time. Intuition seemed like something I'd only be able to honor if I could sit at home and wait until I was hungry to eat, and always had access to the foods I craved. In the "real world", when you're working, going to school, taking care of kids—doing pretty much anything, really—the meals you eat and the content of those meals is not always left up to you. Maybe you're hungry at 11am but your lunch break isn't until 12.30. Maybe you're craving a tuna fish sandwich but the only option at the deli is ham and cheese.

How was I supposed to connect to my intuition if I *didn't*

trust myself? How could I make this work if I *didn't have complete control* over every decision?

What exactly is intuition?

Here's a scenario. Let's say that you eat fast food burgers three times a day, and decide you want to be healthier and listen to your intuition. Do you think that when you wake up the next day, miraculously you're going to crave cabbage? If it's not something your body recognizes, the odds are a strong *no*.

Intuition is based off of past experiences. Build your experiences, build your intuition.

You weren't born knowing what broccoli tasted like until you tried it. There's no way you would ever have the opportunity to crave broccoli if it wasn't for that first taste. In other words, your *instinct* for needing nutrients is there, but your *intuition* guides you to foods you've had based on past experiences.

The road to intuitive eating is not intuitive! If you want to be the kind of person who enjoys healthy foods, you need to actually experiment with trying new tastes, different cooking methods, and an array of seasonings, until your body can completely register if it's something you want to continue having or not.

Be curious

Let me assure you of something. You've never explored how to eat in your entire life until right now. Play with it.

Experiment. Be curious. *You're not going to find the answers through restriction.*

I didn't like foods such as raw chocolate balls or oatmeal when I first tried them. Simply giving myself a chance to experiment with eating them in a way I did enjoy—like starting first with macrobiotic chocolate desserts or cooking the oatmeal in apple juice—gave my body a chance to consider the foods before completely crossing them off a list.

Experimentation is what develops your intuition. Now that you know intuition requires experience with trying new foods and techniques and observing how you feel, what about getting to the point where you just don't have to think about it anymore? Well, that's the next step.

People who eat intuitively all have one thing in common: They don't analyze what goes into their mouth. How is that different from your situation? All the diets you've been on have been entirely about analysis. That's not the way to give you diet freedom; that's the way to create a nice body along with an obsessive mind.

Becoming the kind of intuitive person who eats what they crave when they crave it, then stops when they don't want any more—that doesn't happen from analyzing. It happens from letting go…

Awareness is not the goal

I don't know about you, but I don't want to be aware *all* the time. You *do* need awareness in the beginning to gain understanding and clarity around what isn't working for your health and what new things to try, but constant awareness is not the goal. Instead, the aim is for your eating habits to become second nature. For that to happen, you need to go through the process of experimenting with foods so you can learn what your body needs. You also need to set up your environment in a way where health is not something you have to think about actively.

Let's reflect

I know you wanted to change your body ages ago, but feel confident in the knowledge that *transition* will help in the long run.

1. If you've spent a lot of time eating higher stress foods, then healthier options are going to taste bland. Not only are the foods going to taste unappealing at first, but you'll also have strong cravings for the foods that have been holding you back. Allow yourself to experiment with different kinds of ingredients to allow your body and taste buds an opportunity to adjust.

2. Your current lifestyle and past eating habits have created your current health, which means you're responsible for how you feel right now. Enjoy every bite of the foods you still strongly crave. Ban feeling guilty during your transitional process. You *can* help yourself feel better in the future.

3. Intuition is learned. Your body can only crave what it knows, so be curious and introduce your body to a wide variety of foods. You can't learn from restriction.

4. Constant awareness is not the goal. Use awareness to build your intuition. You will develop a partnership with your body where you can understand its needs and respond in a positive way without having to be mindful all the time.

Part 6: Unexpected Discoveries

Up until this point, we've covered what to consider for your lifestyle and how to transition your diet moving forwards. But you might experience some obstacles along the way, so I'll share with you what can happen after your transformation, and the emotional transition you might experience.

As predicted, my sleep improved, my digestion became regular, my skin cleared, and I had so much energy in the morning that I'd easily wake up before my alarm clock and bound out of bed. Every time I went number two, I'd rub my belly and say, "Good job!" It seemed kooky to say that out loud, but it was a daily acknowledgement that my body and I were finally working together in partnership. My relationship with my body started to shift. Before, it was like I was an uptight parent who, out of frustration, would occasionally let my child run wild. After, it was like a perfect marriage. The kind where I support my partner with what it needs when it needs it to fully thrive. And in return, it supports me even if I'm not always on my game. Even when I'm not the best partner, my body still has my back.

YO-YO DIETER	15 LBS LIGHTER...
I GOTTA LOSE 15 LBS!!!	NOW, WHAT DO I DO!?!

It's hard to dislike yourself when you feel so darn awesome. But even so, there were some experiences I encountered that were unexpected where I had to question my comfort with the changes that were happening.

Unexpected side effects: the bad and the brilliant

Once you reach your goal and your body changes, you

would think you'd suddenly become this new person. That woman who looks good in whatever she wears, is the life of the party, and who can date whomever she chooses. Surely, everything in life will be perfect once your body has changed... *right?*

Changing your body is a big *identity shift*. You've labeled yourself as someone who is chubby, struggles with weight, is unattractive, who will always have to be on a diet, and on and on. So when the day comes that you're actually *not* chubby, you *don't* struggle with your weight, and you're *not* unattractive... it makes you question your self-identity. Changing your body comes with constant daily tests about whether you want to stick to who you *were* or step into who you want to *become*. Who you've become *isn't* who you used to be anymore. Can you handle that?

I look... *great?*

One such example of this was the time I was sitting at the bar playing on my phone while my friend was off to the restroom.

"Hi! Is this seat taken?" a handsome fellow asked.

Oh my gosh, he's gorgeous.

"Oh ummm, no, that's fine, you can sit there. Don't worry, my friend is coming back from the bathroom soon."

"What do you mean?"

"My friend, you, uhh, wanted to talk to her, right? She should be coming back from the bathroom, soon."

"Ha ha! I was waiting for her to leave so I could come talk to *you*."

Wait... me? Oh my gosh. What. Was. Happening!?

Ever since I could remember, I had taken on the role of matchmaker. That odd friend who tags along with a guy and a girl. Guy and girl happen to decide they like each other and give said friend odd looks, wondering why she hasn't politely decided to go do something else.

And now... what was this new unexpected attention? I mean, sure, *thankfully*, my back fat was no longer bigger than my boobs, but didn't he notice my tummy hanging out over my pants while I was sitting down? Or the chin zit that had said hello that morning, because it knew I was going to run into someone hot and always had amazing timing? Maybe he would have approached me if I was at my peak weight. I'll never know. The only thing I knew for sure was that I was getting more attention the more my body changed, so I felt pretty assured there was a correlation.

In general, my body was changing for the better and I continued to feel amazing. But I wasn't prepared for the responses I would get through these changes. People were noticing me.

"Wow, your skin looks so much better!"

"You lost so much weight!"

Even people I had *never met before* would say things like, "Oh come on, eat a bit more, you can afford it." *What?*

You'd think I'd be excited about these compliments, considering how much I wanted to change my body in the first place. Instead, I felt awkward about them. I had started off as someone who was mortified at the idea of people making comments about my weight, and suddenly my weight was something I was being constantly reminded about, even though the comments were positive. I had tried to hide from comments for so long, but I couldn't hide any longer.

What I was confused about the most, though, was why I felt awkward to receive such nice compliments. *Isn't this what I wanted? Didn't I want to be seen as a gorgeous diva?*

The more I thought about it, the more I realized that the discomfort came from the fact that my thoughts about myself—the labels that I had put on myself all throughout dieting—hadn't changed when my body changed. When I looked in the mirror, I didn't necessarily see a slim woman. I saw a chubby woman in a slim body. It dawned on me that the reason I had sabotaged every other diet I'd done in the past was likely because I still held onto the *belief* that I was a yo-yo dieter. I realized that I had to let go of any labels I had for myself if I really wanted to be comfortable in my body and live the lifestyle I envisioned.

And that meant I had to learn *what* made me uncomfortable about these compliments.

What I'm talking about comes down to body image. So, what *is* body image?

Maybe you think body image is about how we feel about

; when we realize that we don't look like a supermodel in a magazine. But it's a bit more than that. Body image is about your self-identity. That means two things:

1. How you see yourself

2. How you *want* to be seen by others (or how you *think* others are perceiving you)

Negative body image usually stems from a disconnect between these two aspects of self-identity. In other words, when your view of yourself doesn't match how others perceive you (or vice versa). This could look like any of the following:

You want to be seen as someone who is *responsible*, but you have a face full of acne and worry that people see your zits and question if you are a responsible person who can take care of herself.

You want to be seen as someone who is *trustworthy*, but the fact that you're a binge dieter makes you question if people can trust you especially when you can't trust yourself.

You want to be seen as someone who is *attractive*, but you overheard your male friend make a negative comment about a woman your size and that planted doubts about your own level of attractiveness.

What I find interesting about body image is that, most of the time, these concerns aren't caused by comments made directly to you. In these examples, maybe no one ever said you're irresponsible because of your acne, untrustworthy because of your bingeing, nor unattractive because of your weight. They are labels we have given ourselves based on our judgements of other people and assumptions we have made from situations we have observed.

I wasn't a yo-yo dieter out of laziness. I was a yo-yo dieter because of an illusion of responsibility. I believed it was more important to look like someone that works hard than to get sleep. I believed it was more important to eat a salad in front of people to look like I cared about my body but then binge in secret. But the more I cared about these things, the more I let the ball drop on my own self-care.

Widening your scope

You might not have many—or any—opportunities to see lots of naked women, but I have. My Japanese family were public bathhouse owners, which meant I often went to bathe with strangers whenever I visited Japan. That meant that I had a chance to see what average women of all ages looked like, from small prepubescent children all the way up to 80-year-old grandmothers. Even amongst Japanese people who you might think have more genetic similarities, there is a wide variety of body types. Round boobs, cone-shaped boobs, bowl-shaped boobs. Tall, medium height, short. Long torsos, thick torsos, short torsos. Long legs, strong legs, short legs. Youthful skin, spotted skin, wrinkly skin. Flat bellies, jiggly bellies, bellies that show signs of giving birth to many children. Birthmarks, moles, scars.

The one thing they all have in common? They're all beautiful. The body is so beautiful at different stages of life, and each mark, shape, color, and wrinkle tells a unique story. The more I saw these variations, the more I felt that surely, just surely, I must also represent a source of beauty.

When you open up a magazine, you see one kind of beauty. When you shop at retail stores, those clothes might be designed with a certain body type in mind. And it's easy to feel excluded when the reality is that you're one of many kinds of beauties, even though you haven't been exposed to them all.

Body confidence means you've reached a point where you can celebrate your own beauty and the beauty of other women without feeling like you yourself need to change. If you want to be more confident with your body image, it starts with two things: it's time to stop making judgements about other people, and it's time to recognize your own role in the scope of beauty.

Fear of gaining it all back

I was so excited to have positive changes with my health, but I was also deathly afraid that it could be taken away at any moment if I allowed myself to somehow slip back into old habits.

One time I was so afraid to travel back home to the US that I took an extra suitcase full of organic cooking ingredients with me so that I could feel like I had some level of control over my food options.

The thing is: worrying about being unhealthy is also an unhealthy mindset. There's even a word for this: *orthorexia*. Since I had never experienced this high level of health and happiness with my body while eating foods from my past, I wasn't sure I could be happy if I slacked, even just a little.

MAY 4th
HEY, WANNA GRAB PANCAKES ON SUNDAY?
SORRY, CAN'T. I'M GLUTEN FREE.

MAY 11th
HEY, WANNA GO TO THE BBQ TOMORROW NIGHT?
SORRY, CAN'T. I'M VEGAN.

MAY 18th
HEY, WANNA GRAB SLUSHIES AT THE BEACH?
SORRY, CAN'T. I'M SUGAR FREE.

MAY 25th

JUNE 1st
WHY DOESN'T ANYONE WANT TO HANG OUT WITH ME?!

Maybe you think you are healthy, but you know you could be healthier. *What degree of healthy is healthy? Am I not as healthy as I could be if I choose to have eggs and rye toast instead of a green smoothie? Am I not as healthy if I have a regular snack instead of one that is gluten-free? Am I not as healthy if I take a nap instead of doing a workout?*

I had been so excited about everything I'd learned, but I was coming across the same issues I'd had in the beginning of my health dilemma: I felt like socializing and living a full life that included cuisine would completely undo my progress. I was terrified of the risk of sabotaging all of the positive things I had done up until that point. I imagined that the second I started reincorporating foods I had cut out, I'd be back at square one.

A client once said to me that sometimes it's easier to be 100% strict than it is to find balance. And that's so true, because every time you have something that's considered not healthy by any standards—even if it contributes positively to a life experience—you feel like you're doing yourself a disservice and don't trust that you'll reach your health goals.

But simply knowing about cause and effect as well as trusting my body helped me find the right balance. It was scary at first to get comfortable with consuming foods I had once blamed for my weight issues, or that were processed or not organic, but I feel emotionally at peace now even if my body and eating habits aren't perfect on paper. It feels good to be comfortable with dining out or open to eating the occasional airplane food out of necessity. In addition, since my tastes and cravings had changed so much, I found that I didn't have to worry about slipping into old habits since those habits had lost their appeal.

Remember: it's all about experimenting until you find that zone where you feel the most comfortable. You *will* find it.

Clothes might not fit how you thought they would

I thought that losing weight would make me look amazing

in any clothing style I wanted to wear. The reality? On one hand, I do feel more open to wearing a variety of styles that I wouldn't have tried when I felt more self-conscious. But there were certain kinds of clothing I had wanted to wear that I realize wouldn't ever look quite how I expected. And that's more because of my body type and less because of my weight.

I grew up in a time when Britney Spears was one of the main idols. I always wondered what it would be like to look great in a tank top and short shorts. But even after I lost weight and could actually wear those tank tops without them stretching in the wrong places, I found that I was still not quite satisfied with how it looked on me, because, well, Britney and I have different body structures.

That gave me more confidence to go to stores and try things on for the sake of finding what fits properly. I became more curious about what clothes looked good on me instead of being frustrated about not fitting into what I thought I should wear.

It was the first time that I realized that the issue was the clothes, how they were cut and sewn, not with the size of my butt. That was certainly freeing, but I didn't have to lose a lot of weight to figure that out.

I encourage you now—no matter what you think of your body condition—to be open to trying many different kinds of clothes purely for the sake of finding the right fit. You'd be amazed at how much your confidence soars when you have clothes on that feel right. You don't have to start with your weight to get that kind of satisfaction.

Self-Validation = Freedom

While wandering the streets of Tokyo, I was scouted for modeling. While I'm nowhere near the height or body structure of conventional fashion models that you might be familiar with, the Japanese fashion industry has a thing for half-Japanese people like me. We tend to be a bit taller than the Japanese population, and in my case I have a more Western body shape, but retain Asian features.

My heart raced as I approached the modeling agency. I took a deep breath as I waited for the double doors to open, and exhaled as I made my way into the building towards the elevator.

This was it. I felt like I was being rewarded for finally being kind to myself and learning how to care for my body. Getting scouted for modeling was like the universe patting me on the back saying, "Good job, girl!"

I got off the elevator and made my way into the agency. The agent had me fill out some forms, asked me about my measurements, had me walk back and forth across the floor, and started talking about what kind of modeling I'd be suited for.

"Yeah, Katheryn, I think you have a lot of potential, but we're not going to sign you until you've lost another five pounds."

A few seconds earlier, she had seemed totally fine and positive about signing me on until I revealed to her my weight. It was as if I *looked* qualified to her eye, but not good enough *on paper*. I wasn't even sure if I believed her because her comment felt so *automatic*, as if that's just how she greeted people as an agent in the modeling world. "Hi, nice to meet you, lose five pounds. Oh, this is your friend? Hi, lose five pounds."

I didn't feel offended, worried, or compelled to change. All I could think was, "Seriously, lady? Are you blind? I look freakin' awesome."

I left the agency with an odd sense of relief. Like I had just avoided jumping into a world that involved more negative self-talk. The kind of self-talk that is never necessary.

As I made my way back into the subway station, it dawned on me: that was the *first* time I had ever stood up for my body. It was the first time that I had given *myself* validation. I didn't need to consult media articles to confirm whether or not I was eating right. I didn't yearn for someone to reassure me of my insecurities with compliments. I didn't feel the need to do five more painful reps at the gym because, well, what was I working towards, anyway? I was working towards *feeling good*.

All of the validation I needed had come from myself in that moment. That was when the curse of years of dieting was finally broken. I was *free*. I floated home like a *girl on bliss*.

Trusting yourself

When you've spent countless years worrying about your weight and trying various diets, trusting yourself seems like the last possible option. If none of these "proven diet methods" have worked, it's much easier to believe that something is wrong with your motivation or willpower. And if you have wild cravings, then listening to your body is the last thing you'd think would get you healthy.

I've also met women who have a wealth of knowledge about healthy foods and who are always picking the best quality options, but they still search for answers to help with cravings and overeating. They don't need to study food and health any more—the last step they're missing is trusting their bodies more than they trust tools and theories at face value.

So, how can you start to trust yourself when you've let yourself believe that you're the problem?

Permission to have a voice

In my case, I couldn't trust myself. My cravings *were* crazy. So I put my trust and faith into nature. I believed wholeheartedly that Mother Nature didn't want me to be unhealthy. I believed in the cycles. I believed in experimenting. I believed that my body knew the answer even though that answer might not be clear right now.

Once I believed that my body knew the answer, and I gave myself permission to have a voice, I started hearing ideas that never would have materialized if I had kept that voice silent. That voice said I was over-exercising, eating foods I didn't really like, and that it's okay to be pampered.

Here's the thing: you're the only one who knows how you feel. You're the only one who knows what your tastes are.

That means you're the final person in the decision-making process about what works for your body. At the end of the day, you're the only one who knows what feels right to you.

If you keep finding yourself making excuses, maybe that method of health isn't the right one for you. Make peace with knowing what doesn't work. Make peace with making things easier for yourself. This is *your* health experience.

Your tastes *will* change

I also used to think that healthy eating meant constantly having to suppress the urge to overeat unhealthy foods. But what I discovered instead is that transitioning my body into a healthy diet actually reduced the appeal of unhealthy foods. I started to find myself having a few bites of cake and stopping—not because I was restricting myself from the rest, but because the urge to finish it no longer existed in the way it had before.

When your body is out of balance and you have strong cravings, doing something like drinking coffee can make you feel like all of the cells in your body are suddenly activated and alive. But when your body is in balance and you don't have any cravings, drinking that same coffee can make you feel like each of your cells are getting a smackdown. A bit can feel enjoyable but the large quantities that once made you feel good can make you feel overwhelmed.

I used to hear idols say that they eat what they want, when they want it. And I used to feel jealous because I thought that it meant they could eat as many "naughty" foods without consequence. Now, as someone who truly *can* eat whatever I want without worrying about my weight, I discovered that the "secret" behind this concept is that my tastes have changed. Back in the beginning, what I wanted was chocolate chip cookies, all the time. What I want now is sometimes a green smoothie, sometimes fish, and occasionally a chocolate chip cookie. What I want now is different from what I used to want.

You have to trust that your tastes will change through the process. And you need to have the courage to be okay with honoring new tastes even though your old habits beg you to come back.

Relax that focus

What you want to have is a "relaxed focus". That means you are on a path, but without any attachment to the destination. The point is you give yourself a chance and you honor your body when you truly have a craving. Your body knows what it needs. Your inner child is smart. Nature is smart. Trust it. Eat more foods and have fun exploring. You will never know until you try. Don't set yourself up with expectations. Relax your focus. There is something bigger and more powerful than you. We're all part of a cycle.

Your feelings matter

True self-love is allowing *your* tastes, your feelings, your experiences with diet to matter. It's about not putting yourself in stressful situations in the first place as far as possible. It's about choosing to allow yourself to feel good. It's less about acceptance and more about *discovery*. Acceptance is settling. But discovery? That's falling in love with yourself.

Feel powerful in your health journey. At the end of the day, the only way of eating that matters is the one that works for you.

You *can* do this. Mother Nature knows what's best. Your body knows what's best. *You* know what's best.

About Katheryn Gronauer

Katheryn Gronauer is a wellness coach and health writer who helps women integrate health techniques with their chosen lifestyles. Her book *Confessions of a Yo-yo Dieter* is a fun relatable story that reveals a perspective on wellness less commonly known to people trying to lose weight. You can easily find Katheryn wandering the streets of Tokyo in search of new cafes, or more simply go to her website girlonbliss.com where she supports women globally.

Made in the USA
Columbia, SC
25 September 2018